To Helen Beth
& Chris
Prov 3:5-6

The
LONG
WAY
HOME

JOHN P. JEWELL, JR.

THOMAS NELSON PUBLISHERS
Nashville · Camden · New York

Copyright © 1982 by John P. Jewell, Jr.

Published in Nashville, Tennessee, by Thomas Nelson, Inc., and distributed in Canada by Lawson Falle, Ltd., Cambridge, Ontario.

Printed in the United States of America.

ISBN 0-8407-5267-9

Contents

Acknowledgements

I am deeply indebted to Reverend Truman Dollar, who first said, "You must write this story." He read the manuscript, contributed very helpful suggestions for improvement, and has been a sustaining force throughout the past few years of my journey home.

I am profoundly grateful to the Lord for the gift of my wife, Judi, who wrestled with me over the issue of whether we would make our story public. Her love for the Master enabled us to decide that perhaps God might be glorified in some way. Son Jaie contributed many hours of duty at the copy machine.

Reverend James L. Kidd and his wife Joann have nurtured us over the past few years and helped in reading the manuscript. Reverend Arthur O. Bickel, who was my supervisor in clinical training, also read the manuscript and made several helpful suggestions.

The interest of Thomas Nelson Publishers in this story and the encouragement of editor Reverend Peter Gillquist and staff have been invaluable.

To the Reader

I feel a sense of urgency about the message of this book. The urgency is probably best described by an experience that tore my heart apart.

Jack was a thirty-three-year-old pastor of a mainline Protestant church. He had gone through the experience of losing his faith, losing his value system, and finally becoming alcohol and drug dependent. Then he lost his wife and two children when he could not or would not overcome his problems.

I had brief contact with Jack when he sought me out, having heard something of my own struggle with lost faith. Our friendship was terribly brief. It lasted only two weeks. The chairman of the Board of Trustees of his church came to my house one morning and said, "I just wanted to tell you that Jack killed himself last night. We found him in his car in the garage. It was carbon monoxide.''

I went upstairs to my den and went to pieces. I had talked to Jack the night before. We had made plans to get together again. He was in a terrible struggle to overcome his addiction and said that he had a glimmer of hope because I had been able to regain the priceless treasure of my own faith.

I wept uncontrollably for some time because I was just a slender thread from having lived his story myself. Only a miracle kept me from the same end. I weep for Jack, for the scores of people like Jack and myself that I have met all over the country. I am brokenhearted for those who have lost their faith and continue to try to maintain a pastoral ministry. I weep for others who exchanged their faith for an empty ''religious humanism'' which masquerades as faith and leaves hollowness and misery in its path.

It is a painful thing to write about turning my back on the faith that transformed my life and brought fulfillment where there had been absolute despair. I forsook my trust in Jesus Christ, my commitment to biblical Christianity, and the passion I had once had to reach others with the story that alone has power to bring hope to people's lives. I spent years wandering in a hopeless maze of theological confusion, shallow fads, and personal turmoil. I preached out of my own barrenness and threw crumbs to the searching hearts that had come for the Bread of Life.

You need to know I have told this story bluntly, but

honestly. You may wonder why I have gone into detail in some places, but I am confident that in the end you will understand why this story had to be told as it happened.

As I wrote this account, I relived every moment of the past twenty-two years of my life. Sometimes the pain of remembering was such that I wanted to stop. The one thing that kept me writing when the heartbreak was intense was a hope that in some way my story might be used by God to touch some life.

If there is another Jack somewhere who might come to know that it is possible to know the living Christ once again and to have the joy of salvation restored, then the wounds of my own apostasy will have found some further healing.

It is with a sense of fear and trembling, yet gratitude, that I invite you to share this journey with me.

1

Threshold

A pretty green-eyed blonde in black leotards caught my eye from across the room. She winked and smiled and made her way toward our table at the Enlisted Men's Club. She carried a set of bongo drums and was beating on them in time to the music the band was playing.

Not my type, I thought. *Pretty, but I don't think I like her.*

I wanted to leave, but my chair happened to be right against the wall and my friend Eddie was blocking my way on the other side. "Let's get out of here, Eddie," I said. "I think that blonde and her friend are headed our way, and I don't care to make friends with them." I was normally the first for a little fun, but this girl's manner attracted too much attention for my liking.

"C'mon, Eddie . . . let's go," I insisted. But Eddie didn't move. He flashed his silly grin at me.

"You jerk!" I hissed furiously. "You set this up!"

But the girls were there. The blonde and her tall, red-headed friend had successfully invaded our table, all the while smiling, giggling, and acting ridiculous.

"Hi, Eddie!" The blonde giggled. "Fancy meeting you here. Who's your friend?"

"John, this is Judi," said Eddie—who had just become my ex-friend.

"Delighted," I offered in my finest sarcastic effort as I tipped my glass of beer toward her in mock politenesss. I did not like not being in control.

Small talk ensued and I remained quiet and let Eddie carry the conversation. I decided to act angry for a bit longer.

She is pretty, I thought.

Judi finally addressed me directly. "So what about you? What are you doing in the Air Force?"

"Defending the country, Judi. What else?" I replied.

She didn't answer and for the first time was quiet. I sensed she was hurt.

"Actually," I said, "I quit college at Northeastern University in Boston after a semester and a half to major in fun. I was going to join the Air Force and see the world. I really wanted to go to Japan or Germany, but here I am at Olathe Naval Air Station. Exciting, huh?"

"Well," she answered, "it's not so bad. Kansas City is just thirty-five miles away, and there's lots of fun there. At least I think so, and I've lived there all my life. I like to have fun, too."

"So I gathered," I replied as I eyed her bongo drums.

"Hey, Marty. Wanna dance?" Eddie said to Judi's friend. They went to the dance floor—the band had finally started to play some more current tunes, like Buddy Holly—and I found myself alone with Judi. I played with my empty glass, and Judi fiddled with the straw in her drink. A moment's silence seemed like an hour. I glanced up as she glanced up.

Back to the silence.

"Well . . ."

"I uh . . ."

We both spoke at once.

"What were you going to say?" I asked Judi.

"No . . . you first."

"I was going to ask you if you wanted to dance," I said.

She laughed. "Me, too."

We danced and exchanged information. I went to high school in Morrisville, Vermont. She went to Westport High in Kansas City. I came from a broken home and was adopted by an aunt and uncle. She came from a stable home and had parents that cared a lot about her. But they were "religious" and wouldn't like the fact that she was on the base. I asked her if the whole meeting was a set up.

She stopped dancing for a moment. "Yes." She was hesitant, watching for my reaction.

"Why?" I asked.

"Eddie said you were a neat guy and that you liked to have a good time. He said you were tough, too. Did you really take on two sailors?"

"Never mind that. Just stick with the 'neat guy' stuff!"

The evening began to pass rather quickly. After what seemed only an hour, the lights were turned up, and the petty officer behind the bar yelled, "Okay! That's it, you guys . . . get out. Time's up!"

"Nice meeting you," I said to Judi. "See you around, huh?"

"Yeah," she replied. As she and Marty walked to the parking lot, it almost seemed as though Judi was trying to hide her bongo drums.

As we walked back to our barracks, Eddie said, "So whad'ja think?"

"What do you mean?" I answered.

"What did you think of Judi?"

"She's okay. And I know you set this whole thing up. Don't do me any favors, Eddie. I can take care of myself —okay?"

"You know when I danced with Judi?" Eddie continued.

"Yeah."

"I told her that you didn't like her," Eddie said.

"So what?" I replied.

"She said she's going to marry you!" He laughed.

I stopped in my tracks. *"Bull!"*

There was a Halloween party a few weeks later at Judi's apartment, and I received an invitation—via Eddie. I decided to go because it sounded like great fun. I would keep to myself the fact that I had to admit to a slight interest in Judi. We ended up talking quietly in a corner while the party roared on all around us.

"Something tells me there's more to you than meets the eye," I tried cautiously.

"Is that good or bad?" Judi replied. Something in her face told me we were in the process of deciding just what our relationship was going to be like. She seemed genuinely anxious to know what I would say.

"Well," I began, "I'm getting a bit tired of all this running around. I've been stationed here for just over a year now, and there must be more to it all than raising Cain with the guys."

She just smiled.

I called her the following Monday, and we were seeing each other three and four times a week by Thanksgiving.

I borrowed ninety-five dollars to buy a 1950 Ford so I could travel back and forth from the base to Kansas City. We still took in a few parties, but most of our time was spent on quiet dates. There was something compelling about Judi that went beyond the coquettish girl I had met at the club. Her roommate Marty had moved back home, and Judi was saying no to the parties the two of them had been famous for.

It was at Milton's, a small club on Main Street where they played soft mood music, that we both admitted to a tiring of the "fast" crowd.

"I'm sick of the late nights and the parties," Judi said, watching closely to see my reaction.

"Me, too," I agreed. "What's a nice girl like you doing in a place like this, anyway?"

We laughed a bit awkwardly. Our relationship seemed to be turning into something that neither one of us had bargained for.

Judi responded, "I grew up in a really strict home, and I suppose I just wanted to see a little more of the world. After all the 'don'ts' and 'must nots' I wanted to try some of those things for myself. I thought beatnicks were cool."

"That would account for the leotards and bongo drums," I mumbled.

"What did you say?" she said as she slapped my hand.

"Nothing much," I said. "I was just thinking out loud."

Back at the base, my old friends were wondering what was happening to me. "Hey, I hardly see you anymore, Jewell. What's going on with you? Are you going to marry Judi?" my roommate Tony asked.

"No, man—of course not," I replied, but deep inside I knew that I *was* involved. The sure tip-off was Judi's request that I meet her parents. Then came an invitation to attend church with her family.

"Oh, and when you meet them, John, please watch your language, okay? My parents are pretty religious," Judi said. Although she tried to sound as though this were a very casual remark made in passing, I had the feeling there was much more to it.

I remembered an incident that had happened on one of our first few dates. I became angry for some reason and picked up a Bible that sat on the coffee table in her living room and threw it across the room. Judi quickly scooped it up and ran to her bedroom. She didn't come out for fifteen minutes. When she did return, I could see she had been crying—hard, because her eyes were red and puffy. I apologized, but inside I was perplexed. *Why in the world would someone get so upset about a book?* I thought.

Somewhere between Thanksgiving and Christmas, there came the understanding that we were going to get married. I was planning a trip to Ottawa, Ontario, to see my father and stepmother over New Year's.

"You should come with me, Judi," I said. "You can meet my dad, and we can tell him we're getting married."

"But you haven't asked me to marry you, John," she countered.

"Oh, I'm sorry. Will you marry me?"

"Yes," she answered, "but somehow this isn't the way I've always dreamed about being proposed to!"

On the way to Ottawa, I picked up another clue about Judi's inner fiber that startled me. We were changing buses in Detroit when an old man walked up to me and handed me a piece of paper. He was mumbling phrases like, " 'I am the way and the truth and the life' . . . . Do you know Jesus Christ as your personal Savior?" I was extremely uncomfortable, and I didn't appreciate his pushy nature.

When we were settled on the bus I exploded. "What a weirdo! How do you like that old geezer talking all that religious crap to me!"

Judi glared at me. "I wish I had his courage!" she said, then turned away.

Boy, she does have a peculiar streak, I thought. *She must have gotten it from her parents. I'm going to make sure I never discuss religion with her.*

Her funny streak wasn't all bad, though. I wanted my

kids to go to Sunday school, so having a wife with a religious bent would be helpful. After all, I reasoned, a little religion never hurt anybody . . . and heavy on the little. Judi could take care of going to church, and I would have a peaceful, empty house on Sunday mornings where I could browse through the newspaper and pat the dog.

As the bus wound its way toward Ottawa on that snowy night, my mind wandered back through the memories of my childhood in Canada. Judi was asleep with her head on my shoulder, and I wiped the mist from the window so I could watch the huge, puffy flakes racing past my window toward the ground. The snow and the night touched a deep inner chord that came from out of my younger years. Tears began to fill my eyes, spill onto my cheeks, and run down my face. Maybe it was the tenderness of the Christmas season or the pain of some Christmas past, but I was surprised at the intensity of what I was feeling. An old familiar pain filled my insides. A scene from the past came to my mind, and a scab was knocked from some internal wound and it started to bleed again.

I could see a two-year-old child standing at the window of the local beer parlor. He was clad only in diapers, and his face was in need of a good scrubbing. His hands were cupped over his eyes as he pressed his face against the glass, looking intently for someone inside. A man walked behind him and started to open the door to the place. The little guy reached out to stop him and said, "Tell my mommy to come here!"

"Your mother is in there?" he asked quizzically.

"Yes!" he answered, gesturing excitedly. "Yes, tell my mommy to come here!"

I was standing just a few feet away and was unable to get to my brother Brian in time to stop his words to the stranger. I was filled with shame and wanted to disappear from the face of the earth. But the worst was a sudden consciousness of an incredible feeling of loneliness. It made my heart ache again as I remembered it.

"Come on, Brian," I said as I took him by the hand. "Let's go home and I'll fix you some lunch. Mommy won't come home." I was twelve years old.

Dad was gone most of the time with his job as a mining engineer and geologist, and Mom must have been terribly lonely. She drank heavily and became an alcoholic. I remember my parents' late-night fights, and weeks on end when dad was gone and Mom was rarely home, and always, always that biting loneliness.

One night in particular haunts me. Mom and Dad were both at home, but getting ready to go somewhere. I don't remember both of them ever being at home with us for a whole evening doing whatever it was a family would do. This night I was afraid to be alone and afraid to tell my dad that I was afraid. He must have heard my quiet sobbing, because the door to my bedroom opened and he came and sat on my bed.

"What's wrong?" he asked.

"I'm afraid," I replied.

"Oh, don't be afraid, Johnny. You're a big boy now," he said, trying to comfort me. He pressed a quarter into my hand and patted me on the head and told me that everything would be okay. Then my parents left, and I was afraid and alone.

I was shivering and feeling the emptiness of the house and an emptiness down inside somewhere. I cried myself to sleep clutching that quarter in my hand. To this day, when I am quiet and alone, I can still feel the loneliness and fear of that kid clutching his quarter.

As we rode along, I wondered if these memories of my younger years were the reason I had always felt as though my life was a puzzle. I would come so close to putting it all together and then discover there were missing pieces.

Mother left us when I was in eighth grade, and my brothers and sister were scattered to various relatives in the United States. I didn't know why she left. Dad didn't explain. I could feel an incredible pain emanating from him.

Is there anything, I wondered, *that can heal this deep inner sadness I feel?*

The bus labored on through the wintery night, and I could almost feel dad's quarter in my hand again. I wondered why the tears kept coming. I tightened my grip on Judi, and finally drifted off to sleep somewhere east of Toronto. Although I could not perceive it at the time, the arms I had longed for desperately all my life were just beginning to enfold me.

Our trip to Ottawa was marvelous. Dad's new wife, Peg, was accepting, warm, and generously glad for Judi and me. I was overjoyed for Dad because Peg obviously made him so very happy. She and Dad had been married less than a year.

Despite my having few times alone with my father when I was growing up, I did receive from him a deep love for nature and the same sense of honesty he was so well known for. "Your dad could have been a rich man if he were crooked," one of his friends in the mining industry once told me. His blessing on our marriage was important to me, and I had a sense of happiness over the fact that he became very fond of Judi.

"Happy New Year," we toasted, "and to our coming marriage." But would the new year quiet my restlessness, too?

2

The Change

Judi moved home with her parents after our trip to Canada so that she could save some money before we were married. I was getting to know her family quite well by virtue of the fact that I spent most of my free time there.

The intimacy and love that was evident in the Whitts' home was something I had never seen before. I enjoyed everything but church, which came with the territory. Even that was okay, although I could not quite identify what it was that made me so uneasy at times. The meaning of faith for these people was unlike anything I had encountered. It was as though this Jesus actually resided with them in their home.

I was afraid of such intimacy, at least in some ways. Love and closeness always had been intermingled with pain in my life. Everything I had loved wound up being lost to me. My mother, father, brothers, and sister were all taken from me by something I didn't really understand. All I knew was that to really commit yourself to love meant getting hurt.

The Jesus these people knew was a Jesus who was obviously intimate with them. I wanted that and I was afraid of it at the same time. To my relief, Judi seemed to have an uncanny knack for knowing when I needed closeness and when I preferred distance.

Frequently, when I returned to the base in the evening after being with Judi and her family, I would lie awake thinking about what it was they had. Theirs was more than just a happy home. My old idea of fun was not fun anymore. Now I felt empty. When we sang hymns around the piano at the Whitts, I sang right along, even though I didn't have the foggiest notion what the words were all about.

I believed in God. I probably would have said I believed Jesus was the Son of God, whatever that meant. But it was as though they knew Jesus just as they knew me—as a person—and I knew about Jesus just as I knew about Abraham Lincoln or George Washington. Why this difference? I had joined a church, once, when the minister of the Congregational Church in Morrisville, Vermont had come to our house to enlist my aunt as a member. I was on the way out the door when my aunt said to me, "Johnny, do you want to be a member of the church?"

"Sure, why not? What do I have to do?"

"Just sign this," the minister said as he handed me a pen and a piece of official-looking paper.

I signed.

That was it. He shook my hand and I was in! I do think he said something like, "Welcome."

I went to church occasionally after that, and even signed up to teach a Sunday school class so that my girl friend's mother would think more highly of me. But she didn't, and I eventually gave up the class. On those occasions when I did sit through a worship service, I never could figure out what it was supposed to be all about.

I did assume, however, that my church activity was earning me some "points" with God. It made sense to me that enduring the boredom of church was some kind of payment for my sins.

One evening Judi and I were together with her family when the conversation turned to Christ. My palms were sweating, and I began to feel quite uncomfortable. I thought about making an excuse about feeling badly and going back to the base. I would call Judi later and tell her we weren't meant for each other.

My heart was beating so loudly I was sure they could all hear it. Whoever Jesus was, He was calling for some kind of response from me and I didn't understand it. Suddenly I blurted out, "I'm sure if something happened to me on the way back to the base tonight, I'd go straight to hell!"

They all looked at each other. Judi began to cry, and her sister Sandra joined in. Her mother said to the ten-year-old, "Sonny, go out to the car and get my Bible." And Mr. Whitt took the children to the dining room to pray.

I sat there shaking. I was saying in every way except

with the words, "Please introduce me to this Jesus so that I can know Him, too!"

I found myself on my knees before the living room couch with Judi's mother patiently guiding me through the Scriptures. My "points" with God were absolutely useless. I needed the grace and love that Jesus Christ provided for me on the cross. Something from the very depths of my existence told me this was the love I had been longing for all of my life.

I gave my life to Christ.

With a short prayer I invited Jesus Christ to be the Lord of my life, and I ended that prayer with the plea, "And please, Jesus, don't ever leave me alone!"

As I rose to my feet, I felt hundreds of pounds lighter. Everyone was crying, and we were laughing and they were hugging me. I could not remember being cared for like that in my whole life. There was a Spirit that filled the house, and I could feel it. I knew for certain that something eternal had taken place, for I was experiencing a freedom and a joy that was simply impossible to express. I was released from the bondage that had plagued my life.

I felt free to love in a new way too. As I looked at Judi and hugged her, I felt free to love her in a new way that I could not describe. I kept trying to tell the family what I was feeling, but it just came out, "I . . . I feel . . ."

And they would say, "I know . . . I know."

When we had finished laughing and celebrating, I wanted to know more—immediately. "Show me more!" I said. Judi's parents could hardly keep up. We went through the discourse in John 3 about new birth and on to St. Paul's statement in 2 Corinthians 5:17 about becoming a new creature in Christ.

"It's all so clear!" I exclaimed. "How come I never saw this before?" I was absolutely amazed that this Book was suddenly addressed to me personally. I looked at Judi and a sword went through me as I recalled throwing her Bible across her living room.

It was a very long night for the Whitts. I did not want to go home. I wished I could send a message to the base saying I would not be back. Finally, I did say good night, with the understanding I would be back the next night to look at more Scripture together.

On the way back to the base, I sang and shouted and waved at several perplexed motorists along the way.

It was 3:30 in the morning by the time I got back to my room at the base, and Tony was snoring like a buzz saw. I had been looking forward to telling him about my newfound faith in Christ. Tony didn't know Christ any more than I had when I left the base that evening, and I was anxious for him to hear the good news. I slammed the door to our room a couple of times, but to no avail.

I couldn't wait. I shook him. "Hey, Tony! Guess what? I got saved, man!"

Nothing. He didn't budge.

I was really concerned for Tony. We had been friends since our days at school in Biloxi, Mississippi, at Keesler Air Force Base. I thought about one night when Tony and I were driving back to the base from Kansas City after a hard night on the town. As I rounded a curve much too fast, the door on the passenger side of the car flew open, and Tony flew out like a sack of potatoes.

I brought the car to a screeching halt and ran back to where Tony had disappeared into a wheat field. I was sure he was dead. But then I heard him laughing. He had thought it was the funniest thing in the world.

Now I was concerned about Tony's life in a new way. "Hey, Tony! Wake up, man! *Tony*!"

He was beginning to stir.

"*Tony*! . . . *Wake up*! I met Jesus Christ tonight, and I want you to meet Him too. Get up, Tony. I have to tell you this!"

Groaning, Tony rolled over and winced at the light I had turned on so I could show him some Scripture.

He rubbed his eyes and yelled, "Whadda you want?"

"I got saved, Tony!"

He wasn't impressed. "Aw, c'mon, Jewell, go to bed, will ya? You'll feel better in the morning." He rolled over and was back to his buzz saw in a few seconds.

But it was quite some time before I could settle in. My heart was full. Sleep came to me that night with a sense of the peace I had been looking for all my life.

3

Where To From Here?

I have a tremendous sympathy for the apostle Peter, who wanted to build a monument on the Mount of Transfiguration. The mountaintop of coming to know Christ was the most beautiful height I'd ever known. I thought I would remain on that lofty peak forever.

Living on the mountaintop brought with it an insatiable hunger for Scripture. I was reading the Bible every spare moment. With enthusiasm, Judi and I attended the large church her parents belonged to. I carried a pocket New Testament to work and read whenever I could.

By the time we were married (Judi and I moved our wedding date up to April), I had read through the entire Bible once and was working through it again, this time with a commentary. We settled into a delightful little apartment in Kansas City. Judi worked in the city, and I commuted to the base. But my mind was overwhelmed by one thing: the Word of God. Each page held new revelations, which I would rush to share with Judi—who was becoming more and more impatient with my Bible reading.

I could not understand why Judi was not as excited about all these startling discoveries as I. She, on the other hand, could not understand why I was not more excited about her than I was about Christ and the Holy Scriptures.

About sixteen days into our young married life, I went rushing into our bedroom to bring Judi a tremendous new insight from Isaiah 53. Abruptly she interrupted me. "John, are you the same guy who suggested to me not so long ago that my parents were overly religious?"

"You wanted me to become a Christian, didn't you? And aren't Christians supposed to study the Bible?"

I felt guilty as the words left my mouth. Mountaintops are beautiful, and all of us need them. But I was on my way down for the first time.

Along with my descent of the mountain came my very first questions and struggles. I began talking to one of the guys at the base who was known as the "intellectual" of our crew. Ted was a quiet, studious sort who read voraciously. He told me he was an atheist, and although I differed with him strongly, I had a great deal of respect for his learning. In a few weeks we were discussing Kafka, Camus, and some of the philosophers who rejected the theistic world view.

A process began here that is very important. My zeal

for worship at the church sagged, and my personal spiritual discipline fell behind. The spark went out of my Bible reading, as I turned my attention to other writings. Providentially, I was reading some philosophy one evening when I had a sudden recollection of my old emptiness and inner loneliness. I was jolted back to my senses. The spectre of the old despair and fear was enough to make me rush back to the fellowship of the church, where I found help in continuing my Christian growth.

Judi and I were both teaching Sunday school, and I was asked to become superintendent of the high school department. I found myself thinking that I wanted to do absolutely nothing with my life but work for Christ.

I don't remember for certain the very first time the idea entered my mind, but I was drawn to the preaching ministry. My own heart burned whenever I listened to the pastor of our church. My struggle was with the kind of person I thought myself to be. *What in the world would Jesus Christ want with someone like me?* I wondered. When I hinted vaguely at my desire to preach, Judi's response was so cool that I had my own reaction of inadequacy reinforced.

"I don't want to be a preacher's wife," she said with conviction.

There was one thing Judi really did want to be, however. She came home from a doctor's appointment one afternoon with a look on her face I had never seen before.

"Guess what?" she said.

"What?" I answered.

Judi just patted her stomach and raised her eyebrows mysteriously.

"Come on, Judi . . . what?"

Pat, pat, pat. Her eyebrows went up and down again and she chuckled a bit.

"Come on, Judi, tell me! I can't stand this. Why are you patting your stomach?" I knew and I was delirious inside, even though we had decided we weren't going to have children for seven years.

She stretched it out for what seemed an eternity. "We . . . are . . . going . . . to . . . have . . . a . . ."

"Baby! Baby!" I yelled.

"Oh, yes, John! I know it's too early. Are you mad?" she asked.

"Yes," I said as I picked her up and swung her around the living room. "Yes, I'm really furious." We fell to the floor and laughed and cried.

"Oh, Lord, I am so happy!" I cried in an explosive prayer. God's gift to us of a child only seemed to be a greater reminder of His grace.

In my Scripture reading, I was drawn more and more to the accounts of the call of God to men like Moses, Abraham, and especially Peter. Peter was my kind of guy. Impulsive, a fisherman, and as near as I could determine, possessed of a fisherman's mouth. If Jesus could use Peter, I reasoned, perhaps it was not so absurd to think He could use me too.

But how in my current work? I had earned a reputation at the base. The guys had long ago stopped inviting me to the poker games and beer blasts. My old roommate

Tony wasn't the only one who was disgusted. "What's gotten into you, Jewell? You're no fun at all anymore!"

It was interesting, however, that on night duty now and then, a few of the guys would seek me out—when they were sure that no one was watching them. "How come you changed so much, Jewell? What happened? You know I never got much out of church . . . I don't go anymore."

One fellow came during the middle of a long and quiet shift at the radar center. "John, do you think that a person can give whatever talent they have to God?"

"Sure, Dave. I think so. How do you mean?" I answered him.

"Well, I like to sing. Don't say anything to anyone, but sometimes when I feel really good or feel down, I sing and I imagine that I'm singing to God. Do you think that He accepts that?" Dave's sincerity and longing for contact with God seemed to me to come right out of his eyes.

"I'm sure that God accepts that. You know what I think is really important, though? I believe that God wants our hearts. When we give our hearts and lives to Him, then I believe He also wants almost any talent we can offer."

"Is that what happened to you?" he asked.

"Yes. It really is," I replied. "You know how I used to live."

He laughed. "You were pretty wild."

"Yeah. But you know something? People never really see what's going on inside you . . . I always had this terrific feeling of emptiness. I used to wonder what life was all about and what the point of it all was."

Dave was listening intently. "I think that's what my singing is about sometimes."

As the seriousness of the conversation dawned on me, I began to feel nervous. But I plunged on. "What happened to me was that I came to discover that Jesus Christ is for real. I asked Him to enter my life and to fill the loneliness and emptiness I always felt."

"It worked?" Dave asked, almost incredulously.

"Yes, it worked. I didn't become a saint, but I would have to say that these are absolutely the happiest days of my life."

Our conversation ended when Dave had to take the radar scope, but we talked often in the days after that. Some months later he told me that he had gone to church with his girl friend and had given his life to the Lord.

The "Peter" in me came to the fore more often than once, however. One night during a tour of duty, Ted, the intellectual, began to make remarks about the changes in my life. His sarcastic "Well, now that you've seen the light, Jewell . . ." triggered my anger and I snapped back, "You keep rejecting and rejecting, and you're going to find yourself in deep trouble with the Lord. You're going to wind up in hell!"

I felt bad about that outburst and decided to apologize to him the next night. But before I had the chance to do so, he came to me and said, "John, you'll never believe this, but last night on the way home I was possessed with the most powerful fear of God I've ever known! If I weren't a rational, thinking man, I would have been totally and thoroughly converted.''

He took his fear to be a childish projection of some inner psychological weakness. I was convinced once again of the reality of the work of the Holy Spirit. He dropped the fun making after that, but was unable to get past his intellectual difficulties to the idea of faith in Jesus Christ. He could not surrender his intellect to a Greater Mind.

As Ted struggled with his intellectual doubts, I continued to struggle with the compulsion to give myself totally to Him. I wanted to give myself to Him completely, but what to do with Judi? I had not dared to approach her again on the subject.

In December, we attended a series of services in a small Baptist Church near our home. The building was small, but the power of the Spirit was tremendous. Each evening the conviction grew within me that I must offer my life to Christ for His service in a public way. There was an opportunity to do that at the close of the last meeting. Appropriately, the preacher had spent the whole evening on Isaiah 6:8, "Whom shall I send, and who will go for us?" (KJV).

A thousand voices churned and debated within me. "Go! Do it! He means *you*!" But what about Judi?

Judi had positioned herself in the seat by the aisle and I was against the wall.

The hymn of invitation continued. "*Just as I am, tho*

tossed about, with many a conflict, many a doubt . . ."

I could not sing. A cold sweat broke out on my forehead.

"Fightings and fears within, without . . ."

Fear and conflict? There was a war going on down inside me. The baby was coming. I had planned on going back East to college to become a teacher. This would mean so much change. Yet, there was no real choice. I simply did not want to do anything with my life except to tell the story of this Christ who so filled my emptiness.

Judi's hand was on my arm as though to still the shaking. *She wants me to sing, to get my mind off what is going on. She intends for me to calm down and sing so that we can go home and get back to normal.*

"Do something, John," Judi whispered.

". . . Oh Lamb of God, I come, I come!"

I was gone. *Judi's reservations will have to be Your problem, Lord*, I told Him as I headed for the front of the church.

The relief was immediate as I surrendered to the powerful invitation to the harvest. I was filled with a passion to tell the world about this fantastic, liberating love. As I finished praying with the pastor of that church to cement my decision, I looked to my side and there was Judi, kneeling and praying with tears streaming down her face. She had come to give herself to Christ once again.

My mind was reeling. In a few short months I had seen the reality of the supernatural so clearly and the power of the Holy Spirit working so vividly that I would surely never doubt His power again as long as I lived . . . would I?

I turned my attention to preparing for the ministry. Judi was so committed to our future together that I was amazed at how God had provided a way, in spite of the objections and reservations we raise when it comes to placing Him first in our lives. I was granted an early discharge from the Air Force, and the future seemed bright and certain.

On April 11, 1961, we scaled another mountaintop when Judi woke up and said, "John, I think this is it!"

I shook from the moment we left the house to get to the hospital until the doctor came to tell me that I was the father of a terrific 9 pound, 11 ounce boy. "John Patrick Jewell III"—"Johnny."

I was able to see Judi as she was wheeled out of the delivery room. She looked to me like the most beautiful woman in all of creation. My tears even felt good as I said to her, "Isn't he beautiful, Judi? I want to give him all the love and the care and the homelife I didn't have."

The joy he brought to our hearts was unspeakable. The pain he would one day bring, unimaginable.

4

I Love to Tell the Story

A passion was kindled within my being to tell the story of Jesus Christ. This passion burned so, I thought it must have been what Cleopas and his friend had experienced on the Emmaus Road, "Did not our hearts burn within us . . . ?" (Luke 24:32).

It seemed that life now at long last was firmly planted in something permanent and beautiful. Life offered a peace and a sense of direction for me where two years earlier there had been only an elusive longing of my heart. At long last, I was finding the missing pieces of the puzzle!

I longed so to tell this powerful story. I studied, prayed, read the lives of the great preachers, and hung on every word that was spoken from the pulpit of our church. "Oh, Lord," I prayed, "it seems like an eternity

41

will pass before I get to proclaim the glories of Your love."

A couple of weeks after I prayed, the opportunity came. A friend from church was an insurance agent for a pastor who served a rural church. This pastor was going to take a trip and needed someone to preach at the Wednesday evening prayer service.

"Would you be willing to take that service for him?" this friend asked.

"Why sure, Glen," I said in my most calm, matter-of-fact voice. In the depths of my soul, I was singing, "Thank you, God! Glory halleluia! Praise the Lord!"

I had about a week to prepare my ten-to-fifteen-minute sermon. I spent every waking moment with my attention focused on that Wednesday evening service. I scolded myself for fantasying that this little sermon could ignite the modern Great Awakening. Then in my next thought I prayed my tongue wouldn't be stopped like Zacharias's was in Luke 1.

I wrote and rewrote that sermon fifteen times. While I was on night duty at the base, I preached the sermon in my mind. When I had the radio monitor, I would preach it out loud. The radio monitor sat in a large, soundproof room to monitor the communication of military aircraft in the vicinity, separate from where the rest of the radar crew worked. I took the opportunity to transform the place into a small church. On one occasion I preached my sermon with what I thought was a good deal of passion. When I finished, I was stunned to hear applause and two or three loud "Amens!" Apparently one of the guys had opened the door. Upon hearing my practice session he had run to get three or four of the men to come listen in. I was devastated, and it was a week or so before I said very much at work. I never did preach another sermon there.

The prayer service was exciting. The second Great Awakening didn't begin then, but neither was I tongue-tied. I was asked to come back and preach on Youth Sunday. My passion for telling the story did not abate. It grew and multiplied.

Judi was totally absorbed in her new role as a mother. We spent hours in the evening playing with Johnny and simply staring at him when he slept. We talked about how we would live when I started school at Calvary Bible College. Though our hearts were full, our pockets were quite empty. With a wife and a child to support and tuition to pay, I wondered just how we would survive.

God answered my wonderings in a way that taught me just what it means to trust Him for provisions for our journeys of faith. My own nature is to want to have a well-stocked storehouse; God was about to teach me to depend on Him. I wanted to store up my daily bread; He was going to teach me to live on the manna He provides when it is needed.

Our pastor called me to his office and told me that the church custodian was leaving. Would I like to have the job? Before I was able to calm the burst of excitement that filled me, he added, "John, there's a little house on the hill behind the church that we're thinking of buying. It needs an awful lot of work, but if you are willing to work on it with some of the men in the church, it is yours to live in while you are in school and working here.''

Tears filled my eyes. Now I knew why Zacharias couldn't speak. It was joy—holy joy. I did manage a "Thank you!" which came from the bottom of my soul.

The process of restoring that little house turned into a marvelous experience. Several men from the church came to help. The fellows on the church staff assisted, and when the weather was willing, the women brought food and we picnicked in the church yard during lunch break.

Room by room and board by board, inside and out, that tiny house became a new dwelling place, transformed by the work and the love of the people of our church. In passing, one of the staff remarked, "John, this house is very much like your life, isn't it? Your life has been overhauled by Jesus Christ in much the same way that we're overhauling this house."

Summer passed. We moved into the house, and I began classes at Calvary Bible College in Kansas City. Although Judi had gone back to work just two weeks after Johnny was born, she was able to take a couple of months off and be at home after we moved into our little house on the hill behind the church.

There were opportunities to preach at various churches in those first months. But the most powerful experience of my early years in ministry was one Sunday evening when the pastor at our home church was away and our associate pastor was not available. When the call came to ask me to take the evening service, the opportunity literally made me catch my breath. I got on my knees in the pastor's study minutes before the service and asked for God's mercy. *I'm not ready for this responsibility, Lord,* I prayed. Our evening service had an attendance of about seven hundred people, and the opportunity overwhelmed me. It was with fear and trembling that I went into the pulpit that evening.

As the service was drawing to a close and we sang a hymn of invitation together, these words leapt to my mind: ". . . when he saw the multitudes, he was moved with compassion on them, because they fainted, and were scattered abroad, as sheep having no shepherd" (Matt. 9:36 KJV).

Suddenly I was overcome with love for these people. It was as though pain and brokenness for that whole congregation came over me. Then there were waves of the Holy Spirit's love flowing through the whole place. Something was stirring and moving in our midst that was not at the command or behest of any of us. Jesus Christ simply walked in our midst through the power of the Holy Spirit. That night was one of the most humbling experiences of my life.

The experience of coming to know Jesus Christ, and then of knowing deep within that my purpose in living was to tell the story of His love, had given to me the gift of solid foundations for faith and ministry.

These foundations were simple, but powerful: The reality of the supernatural, the real work of the Holy Spirit in the lives of individuals, the power of the new birth to transform human lives, Scripture as the Word of

God, the enlivening of Scripture for our nurture by the Holy Spirit, and a deep inner conviction of a specific call to preach the gospel.

These foundations are the crucial building blocks that come alive in the context of the church of the living God. Without these essential foundations we build on sand.

Why in the world would someone who had built his house on a rock want to turn around and build on sand?

5

The Lure of the Far Country

I have always been intrigued by Jesus' parable of the prodigal son. Why would a young man want to take a rich inheritance and squander it away in a distant land? I suspect he had no intention of winding up in difficult straits. Somehow something in the lure of that far country caught a blind spot in that young man's vision and turned his heart from his true home.

I was happy at home. "Home" was the fellowship of our church and the work with our teen-agers. It was classes at Calvary where I was taking in all I could learn like a dry sponge soaks up water. Home was our house on the hill that love had built. It was Judi basking in her dream of a lifetime: a house, a family, and lots of love. Home was my relationship with Christ.

Then a voice from out of my past began the first

whispers of discontent with my spiritual home. Many years ago my father had said to me, "Johnny, even if you want to be a bum, at least be a bum with a degree!" His own education had been hard won, and it was important to all of us growing up. My leaving Northeastern University had pained him.

That voice was activated by a discussion going on in our Old Testament class at Calvary. One of the students mentioned an article in the newspaper about some archaeologist who had turned up remains of a human skull. The scientific conclusion dated these remains as at least one hundred thousand years old.

"Oh, they probably just dug up some old cow bones," the professor quipped jovially.

Almost everyone laughed.

Wait a minute, my mind continued, *that's not really a funny issue. How old is the planet? How do the findings of modern science and our faith relate?*

That event combined with my dad's words about being a bum with a degree became a termite in the foundations I had solidly built upon. I began to pay more attention to the casual comments of other students and some of the pastors in the fellowship our church was a part of. There was a serious anti-intellectual bent to some of these remarks. There was also a deepseated suspicion of learning. "It's what ruined the Pharisees, you know," one pastor said. There was profuse quoting of Paul's, ". . . hath not God made foolish the wisdom of this world?" (1 Cor. 1:20 KJV).

One evening, a prayer service brought my wondering

to a point of real inner conflict. Our music director, who also served as the staff person for our young adult department, was conducting the preaching portion of the service. He told us that he had been asked by a member of the church if he had read a certain new translation of the Bible.

"Why, no," he replied. "There's enough salvation for me in the King James Bible! I don't need any new translation." He continued to tell us how new ideas and serious inquiry were anathema to him. He delighted in his ability to look at only his closed system. "Why, I am so narrowminded," he proudly proclaimed, "that two of me could sleep in a twin bed!"

Some thought his remark was funny. There was some light laughter. Many did not respond at all. I thought it was patently absurd. As an aspiring new pastor, I was taken aback. *How in the world could someone be proud of ignorance?* I wondered.

I remembered our senior pastor making the remark that it would be better to be as ignorant as a hog than to be a liberal. I began to wonder if these were the two choices. What I was experiencing suggested to me that it was necessary to lay down one's mind and one's intellect in order to be spiritual.

Although there had never been a statement that questioning was wrong, there was a silent agreement at the college that we would not question certain vital doctrines of the faith. One could quite easily fall into being "suspect" if too many questions were asked.

I had read some books by a well-known evangelist who

suggested that the torment of hell might not necessarily consist of literal fire that burned the flesh of the screaming tormented. That theory registered very powerfully with me. I was almost relieved to come upon his opinion. Some of the talk I had heard about the torments of hell smacked a bit too much of personal anger and hostility for me. I wondered if such teaching was a projection of anger onto persons whom they did not care for.

I took the question to the associate pastor of our church. He was a friend and had received a degree in a secular university. He was highly respected by the people of our church and admired as a person of intellectual acumen and integrity. I was sure he would be open to my inquiry.

"You know," I said, "I've been struggling with something. I'm wondering if hell really has to be a place of actual fire, where people literally are suffering third degree burns all over their bodies."

His response was very guarded. "John," he said, "you'd better not let some of these guys around here hear you talking like that or they'll never trust you!"

I knew he was concerned about me and his caution was a sign that he cared for me. But I was troubled. We never did discuss the heart of my question. The intimation I drew from our encounter was understood very clearly. Personal struggles with theological issues had to be conducted alone, in the secret of one's own heart. Struggle and doubt were not to be acknowledged openly. This was particularly true for those of us preparing for the ministry. Honest questions were treated as sin. So I buried my questions and intellectual struggles.

The problem is, when you bury things that aren't dead, they ferment under the surface. My questions continued. *Why did God give me this brain if I wasn't supposed to use it?* As I studied the life of St. Paul, it seemed to me that the apostle was able to hold his own very well with the Athenian philosophers. Was the giving of my intellect to God the same thing as sacrificing my intellect for the sake of suspicious brethren?

I began to see the whole issue of the intellect in terms of a choice between faithfulness and apostasy. In my journey through the academic community, I met a great number of colleagues who had come from backgrounds similar to my own. The times we talked together always yielded the same discussion. One, it seemed, had to choose between a repressive, brittle, anti-intellectual bent or a liberal, go-with-the-flow, humanistic orientation in theological style.

I wonder if there still aren't countless people who have bought into this dichotomy, some of whom are perhaps students preparing for ministry or even dedicated pastors now serving the church.

There is a strong commitment to the rational, intellectual process in our society. Western people have invested heavily in the scientific process coupled with an optimistic view of the abilities of the human intellect. This leaves committed evangelicals who have invested heavily in the categories of faith and trust in an extremely vulnerable position. The foundation of educational philosophy is that the learning process depends entirely on the human intellect. Thus, faith and trust begin as questionable constructs! In other words, if my faith and my trust in God come before my commitment to the supremacy of the intellectual process, then my intellect is suspect in academic realms. On the other hand, if I have desires that lean toward the intellectual pursuit of wisdom, then my faith is suspect in my faith community.

I finally went to the minister of our church and said, "Pastor, I want to transfer to another school at the end of this year."

"Which school?" he asked.

"William Jewell College in Liberty," I answered.

"I'm sorry, John. But if you go to that school, you will have to give up your job here. I've known young men who went there and became rank liberals. I couldn't support you in this move."

Something within me shuddered. I wanted to earn an accredited degree. The degree I was working toward at Calvary would not be accredited. Yet, I could not afford to lose my job with Judi and Johnny to care for. We would lose the house.

"I will think about it, pray about it, and let you know soon," I said.

The next two weeks were a time of intense pain. I could sense what a powerful loss the fellowship of the people at church would be. Besides, I had seen the need for a "sponsor" for my Christian growth.

"I will stay at Calvary," I said to myself. "The pastor is right. I am too new in the faith. I would be in deep trouble without the fellowship of this church. Yet, I really want a degree from an accredited school. I'm far enough along to avoid the temptations to give up my commitment to the biblical faith."

When Judi and I talked about this we both struggled. We were in a very tenuous position financially. Yet, she was willing to support whatever move I would make. She understood my need for the kind of education I wanted.

"Where are you in your own faith, Judi?" I asked. "What do you think about my leaving this church?"

"I've never swallowed everything whole, John. But I don't have to think and worry and hash it all out. I have my faith in Christ and my family, and that's what's important to me. You have to decide what to do, and I'll be with you."

" 'Whither thou goest I will go . . .' huh?" I said gently.

"That's right, John."

I thanked God for Judi, but my struggle continued without mercy. In my wrestling back and forth with my decision I did think it through, incessantly. The anxiety of the situation began to crowd out my prayer life. I had a feeling down inside that I could not quite identify—a faint hint that I would head for a far country.

When I checked into William Jewell, I discovered that my credit from Calvary would for the most part be transferable.

So what was the rush? I could spend another year at Calvary before having to transfer. But I was still yearning to go.

Was I now thinking of leaving because of the educational issue, or was this an issue of my own pride? My rational self told me that this was a matter of principle. I was making the best choice I could in terms of my education. I would be able to discern the wheat from the chaff and keep my faith intact.

Another part of me, something within, told me I was about to lose something valuable. The idea never surfaced consciously, but intuitively I sensed my analysis of the situation was not quite correct.

I sought the counsel of Judi's parents. It was in their home and through their love that I had come to faith in the first place. They were supportive. Though they affirmed their continuing care for me no matter what decision I made, I could tell something was wrong. What was it?

Pain. The realization hit me. I saw pain in Judi's mother's eyes. It was not evident in her words, nor even in her actions, but I knew she was hurt.

"We'll try to help you in any way we can, John," was all they said.

I went through one final night of tremendous agony. I had to let the pastor know of my decision the next day. There was no sleep for me that night. I walked the floors and found myself caught between two intense desires. I wanted to stay and to keep my job. I wanted to leave and to pursue a higher intellectual goal. Was the issue pride or was it principle? Was I right and the church wrong?

Was I wrong? Or was there no wrong to it? As I paced the floor and worked through the dilemma for the millionth time, I tried to remember every bit of wisdom I'd been able to pick up since my conversion. My mind was spinning.

I roamed restlessly through our tiny house. I could almost feel each nail and every stroke of the brush that had varnished the floors. We loved this place. There was still that one corner behind our hand-me-down couch that hadn't yet received its paint. I had intended to get another quart of blue and never got around to it.

I remembered the comment about how this place was like my life. There was a sense in which it *was* my life.

It was Johnny's life too. He was now sixteen months old. His first steps across this very floor were almost his only steps. He had walked for just that one day, and then it seemed as though he ran from then on.

A large knot formed in my chest and began to move up into my throat. I tried but could not force it back to where it came from. I broke down and fell to my knees and began to pray with an earnest, volatile quality that surprised me. As the night wore on I reached a tremulous peace with the idea that I needed to stay. My life with Christ was just beginning, and there would be time enough later for intellectual pursuits. It would be best for all of us. I sat on the couch, beginning to feel good about this direction, and I started to fall asleep. Then I woke with a start.

"No!" I yelled. "No, I can't do it! I should be able to go to *any school I want*!"

The struggle started all over again—the same old reasoning and confusion. I had just gotten emotional about my experience and was going to stay for that reason. If I thought it through carefully and rationally, it was best for me to leave.

I paced the kitchen floor and then looked up at the clock. Four A.M. I sat at our rickety dinette table and pounded it and cried out the first streak of profanity that had emerged from my mouth since my days in the service. I stumbled shamefully into the living room and fell asleep on the couch.

Somewhere in the vague shadows of my mind hovered the almost imperceptible sense that I was going to lose something very special.

I went to the pastor's office in the morning. "I'll be leaving," I said.

". . . the younger son gathered all he had and took his journey into a far country . . ." (Luke 15:13).

6

How an Inch
Became a Mile

I gathered all that I had together: my wife, my son, my faith, and my theological convictions and foundations, and took all I had to William Jewell College. I declared my major to be Greek with a minor in religion. In retrospect, I would have been better off with physics or chemistry. I began this journey making the commitment to myself that I would not lose even a trace of my passion for the gospel and my intense desire to tell the story of Jesus Christ.

Judi found a job as a secretary with a chemical manufacturing firm in Kansas City, and Johnny went to a baby sitter in Liberty each day. Judi's time was taken with driving to and from work and then picking up Johnny, fixing supper, and taking care of our apartment. I found a job delivering Fuller Brush products for one of their salesmen, and we managed to barely scratch out a living.

The battle at school was enjoined almost immediately. On the very first day of Greek class, the professor responded to one of the student's questions about the Bible by saying, "One cannot study Greek and do very well at it without discovering that the idea of verbal inspiration is indefensible."

When I entered William Jewell, I was committed to the idea that the Scriptures were inspired by God and that they were absolutely authoritative for the life of the church and the life of the saints. It was a part of my spiritual inheritance. I had personally experienced the power of the Scriptures to call me to new life and growth. I had experienced something I could only call supernatural as the Scriptures began to take on new meaning, and I had gained an understanding that surpassed my mere human understanding. My acceptance of the Scriptures as inspired by God was one of the cornerstones in my faith in Christ and ministry to his church.

I began to feel, as some of the other students shared with me, that the aim of the department of religion was to pry us loose from our terribly archaic view of the Bible.

Each night was a wrestling match! What was I going to accept and what was I going to reject? I wanted the skills and insights that the study of biblical languages could give me, but at this stage of my Christian life I could not discern the assumptions and presuppositions that came with those technical skills. I was beginning, in those first weeks of my work at William Jewell, to get the strong impression that some of the faculty carried a big theological chip on their shoulders. You could boil all the ethereal and sophisticated jargon we were hearing down to a fairly simple statement. "Smart people don't believe the Bible!"

Of course, my own great difficulty was that I really wanted to be a smart person. There were many pre-seminary students who, as nearly as I could tell, also wanted to be smart people. They picked up on and imitated the beliefs and prejudices of the faculty.

The theological assault of the religion classes was worse, however. The very first assignment I received in my New Testament course was a harbinger of the next two years. We were to read the foreword and first chapter of Rudolph Bultmann's *Kerygma and Myth*. I did a fantastic job at this first assignment. I not only read the foreword and first chapter; I almost memorized it! I read it once to complete the assignment. I read it a second time trying to find out what in the world it was saying. I read it a third and fourth time with a theological dictionary because I could not believe that it was saying what I thought it was saying!

When I understood Bultmann's theories, I was locked in another battle. Was it time to be thinking about a career as a truck driver or a carpenter—something I could give myself to without having to combat every new idea that came along?

Bultmann's essay read in part, "The kerygma is incredible to modern man, for he is convinced that the mythical world view is obsolete."[1]

I began to comprehend that this world view "modern man" could not accept included: the idea of the preexistence of Christ, the reality of miracles, the atonement, and the resurrection. Of course the idea of the return of Christ in glory was not acceptable to the rational mind, either. I remember one religion professor affirming with a great deal of embarrassment that he believed that Jesus Christ "could possibly" stand upon the earth once again. He was considered a "fundie," he said, by one of his colleagues.

As nearly as I could tell, Bultmann was saying that the gospel is incredible, that is, not credible, to modern man. Yet, my experience with Christ had been credible to me. I had been changed and placed on a whole new dimension in life because of the very thing Bultmann was saying is not credible to us today!

What to do? I thought about leaving the school immediately. But I remembered a comment one of the professors had made about the fear the "fundies" have of the intellect. (Of course, a fundamentalist was anyone who believed what Bultmann said modern man cannot believe.)

How did this jive with St. Paul, who wrote some nineteen hundred years ago that the gospel was "foolishness" and a "stumbling block" to the human intellect? Paul struggled with the *fathers* of Western philosophical tradition! Bultmann's discovery was not new at all, but I did not know that when I was dealing with his assault on the faith I had cherished.

The essence of what he was saying was, "Smart people don't believe the Bible, and smart people don't believe the gospel"—at least not in any way that is recognizable as biblical Christianity.

I was in pain—layers of pain. I wanted to go back to the church that had given me the inheritance I was spending so quickly. Why not go back? I can only answer that question in retrospect. Having left the church with a degree of pride, it was now my pride that kept me from returning. It would have been humiliating for me to hear the words, "See, I told you so!"

I am sure that if someone had come to see me in those weeks when I was struggling and experiencing the grief and pain of a loss I could not fully comprehend, I might have been able to avoid the pitfalls of the rest of my journey. A call or a visit—especially a visit—like that might have brought me home then. But I suppose I can't blame them. I was, after all, the one who left.

I often wonder if that young lad from Luke 15 had any second thoughts when he first left home for that far country. I am sure he must have. I suspect he had too much pride to go back where his critical older brother lived, and he was much too ashamed to face the father.

Judi knew I was locked in a crucial struggle. Occasionally she asked if something was wrong, but I did not let her in on my dilemma. I did not want her to know the depths of the turmoil that was taking place. If I had been totally and unreservedly honest when she asked, I would have had to say, "I think I'm losing it, Judi. I think I'm losing my bearings."

Distance was just beginning to be a part of our relationship. Judi worked and took care of the apartment, cooked meals and took care of Johnny. Sometimes I felt like I was missing out on his growth. He was talking, laughing, and changing so quickly. The sitter told us that she didn't have to toilet train him. "I found him in with my son trying to get his diaper off so he could go to the bathroom!" she told us.

We were so busy. That was partially the cause of the distance. I didn't want to share too much about what was happening in my inner struggle, because I wasn't one hundred percent sure myself what was going on. That was also a part of the distance. We began in ever so slight a way to keep things to ourselves. I did so because of what was going on inside, and Judi so as not to trouble me. She knew I was already deeply depressed.

I didn't have much time for prayer, and Bible study was limited to that critical kind of reading that was required for the classes in Greek and religion. I didn't notice that the fire had gone out of my reading. I was reading the Scriptures for analysis and critique, much like medical students inspect a cadaver. Devotional reading for the care and maintenance of my heart got squeezed out.

We joined a church but found only a place to attend worship. There didn't seem to be any power or Spirit there. The college community by and large went there, and intellectual respectability seemed to be the order of the day. This was my reason for choosing the church. The pastor was bright; his sermons were very stimulating. But nothing ever happened. We did not get involved in the church, and neither Judi nor I developed any deep friendships at the school.

I began to do supply preaching, and both Judi and I enjoyed these times on Sunday. We went to small churches all over the northern part of Missouri. Johnny came with us everywhere. He tried singing during the hymns, spoke out rather freely now and then during my sermons, and enjoyed being the center of attention. During one of my messages he was particularly restless and talkative, so Judi started for the church basement with him. As they were leaving the sanctuary Johnny let out a big, "Bye-bye, Daddy!" He got such a great laugh from the congregation that his two-and-a-half-year-old mind told him that hollering out "Bye-bye" was a terrific thing to do in church. He tried it two or three more times until he got the point that it wasn't such a good idea after all.

We spent one Sunday at Santa Rosa Baptist Church near Pattonsburg, Missouri. We had a marvelous time, and the people were warm and friendly. There was a touch of spiritual home for us that day. We were asked to come back the next week with a view toward my becoming their student pastor. I was excited once again and spent every waking moment of the next week thinking about that little church. Though it seemed like forever, the next Sunday did arrive. After the Sunday evening service, we went to the home of another student pastor and his wife to wait for a call from the church, informing us of the congregation's decision.

As we left the church, I had Judi's hand in mine, and Johnny was looking backward over my shoulder at the congregation as I carried him toward the back door. I felt as though there were a million eyes watching us, and I wondered what they were thinking. *Do we turn and say good-bye? Do we just leave? Should I say, "Hope to see you again"?* My mind was humming.

Johnny took care of the situation. As we were leaving, he shouted a great big "Bye-bye" to the congregation. We could hear the laughter of the people all the way to the car.

It was difficult to pretend interest in the conversation as we talked with the student and his wife who were hosting our anxious wait. But finally the phone rang. We had left the church exactly sixty-three minutes earlier. A deacon spoke. "Brother Jewell, we have unanimously called you to be our pastor. We haven't had a unanimous vote in my lifetime as a Baptist, so it must be the Lord's will!"

I was ecstatic! I developed my early preaching skills and some caring skills while I was there. And it was while I was at this church that I made a kind of half-way covenant with myself: I separated my life as the pastor in this church from my life as a student. The church was an oasis for me, where I was able to preach the gospel and enjoy Christian fellowship. Those people are important to Judi and me to this day. Here, Judi once again had friends to relate to. We moved to a small town near the church to be closer to the people, the first pastor's family to live "on the field" in decades. Judi found a job at the courthouse in the county seat, and things seemed to go better for us during the two years we served that church.

I am sure those parishoners never knew how valuable their love and acceptance were to this young student. In the lifetime of that church, they have helped at least twenty-five student pastors in the most important part of their training: the day-to-day practical living out of the meaning of the gospel through the pain and trial of people's lives.

Meanwhile, back at school we went through the life of Christ minute by minute "de-mythologizing" everything we could find in the New Testament accounts that were so incredible to modern man. The people back at my church must not have been modern people; they had no trouble with the world view of the New Testament. I had long since decided I would not de-mythologize the Bible for people who didn't need or want it demythologized!

As the months passed, it became even clearer that there is an attitude of basic mistrust in the reliability of Scripture which pervades the theological world. That mistrust does not emerge from the study of the Scriptures, but rather is the logical outgrowth of rejection of the transcendent. The liberal scholar begins with the idea that anything supernatural cannot be and is therefore not valid. Our discussions in class rarely included the possibility that the Holy Spirit actually guided and directed the authors of Scripture. The more existentialist scholars like Bultmann assume that the supernatural is a hangover from man's superstitious past and must be retranslated into terms understood by and acceptable to the modern intellect. The unpardonable sin in the academic community is to question the primacy of the human rational, intellectual function.

There's an old saying that might be restated, "When you live in Rome long enough, you will begin to think like the Romans."

The people at our church decided they wanted an "ordained minister," so my ordination was planned for June of 1963—the end of my junior year at William Jewell. I asked my Greek professor to preach the ordination sermon. That was one sign of how my own journey had taken shape.

No longer was I struggling with the issues that had troubled me in the beginning of my time at this school. I had accepted many of the views that I was digesting day after day. I held the line with issues like the bodily resurrection of Jesus, but the foundations of my faith had been damaged seriously. I knew that my view of Scripture had changed, but I was not consciously aware that I had in fact joined those who place the rational, intellectual capacities of humanity at the helm of the life of faith and belief.

I had grown to respect and admire the intellect of my Greek professor, an ordained Southern Baptist pastor. Though I did not fully accept his theological framework, I placed my own faith experience on the foundation of the human intellect. When he spoke at my ordination, he said that I was one of the brightest students he had ever had. I took too much pride in that. I was committed to the pursuit of all the academic respectability I could get.

As my time at William Jewell drew to a close, I began looking for a seminary. A voice inside said, "Go East, young man, go East!"

7

Farewell

Over a hundred people gathered in the yard of the small house we had rented in Maysville, Missouri. People from Santa Rosa Baptist Church, from the courthouse where Judi worked—along with those people who try to attend every sale that is held—waited for the first call of the auctioneer's voice.

"Who'll gimme a dollar," he said as he held up a picture that had hung on our living room wall.

We sold almost everything we had accumulated since we had married except for essentials, which we placed into a U-Haul trailer that was parked on the street during our sale.

Johnny offered his own help as he ran back and forth from the trailer with his toys. "Sell this?" he queried with the excitement of a three-year-old. "Sell this, too?"

The sun was just greeting the western horizon when I went through the house for a last inspection. The yard and house were empty now; the people had all gone home. There had been the last tearful good-byes with people from our church. Clifford Wolf and his wife Wilma held Johnny one last time and with tears in her eyes, Wilma said, "We're especially going to miss you, little Johnny." And to Judi and me, "He is always so happy and excited, isn't he? Johnny's never known a stranger."

Johnny hugged and kissed Clifford and Wilma and then struggled free from Wilma's grasp and ran to the car. He was ready and anxious for the next new experience.

There was a small summer graduation ceremony in the evening at William Jewell with a reception following at the President's house. Our U-Haul trailer was parked in the lot ready to go. When the ceremony was over, we said our farewells to friends and to Judi's parents.

"Why don't you stay tonight and leave in the morning?" Judi's dad suggested.

But I wanted to leave immediately. I felt anxious to leave, to get on with the next step of my academic career. I wanted to avoid any discussions of seminary with Judi's folks. Her mother, in particular, always seemed to have a sixth sense about knowing people's hearts, and I did not want to talk about Colgate-Rochester with her.

I had applied both to Yale University Divinity School and to Colgate-Rochester Divinity School. Yale had offered a scholarship, and I had been sorely tempted to take it because the name had such a ring of prestige. Colgate-Rochester, however, had offered an Ecumenical Fellowship, given to only two students in the country. The honor and the full tuition scholarship plus stipend had made the difference.

When we pulled out of the parking lot, Judi and Johnny were waving. I could see the Whitts waving, and I knew their hearts were broken.

We drove all night and stopped the next day at a hotel in South Bend, Indiana. Judi took Johnny to the room to get settled in while I went to the bar to have a beer. I was now a man come of age, who had kicked off the outdated piety and behavioral rules of the past. I was an Ecumenical Fellow at a respected Eastern Seminary and a magna cum laude graduate of a respectable college.

As I sipped on my second beer, I thought back to the last time I had taken a drink. I was with my old roommate Tony. I thought back to the old emptiness and loneliness that had plagued me for years. A chill ran down my spine. *So now what?* I thought.

The brochure that first attracted me to Colgate-Rochester displayed a sketch on its cover of a good-looking, middle-aged man on the move with a briefcase in his hand. The cover of the brochure said, "Preparing the scholarly man of faith." That was me.

When we arrived on the campus of CRDS, Judi was anxious to see where we would be living. I secured a key from the office and went to our building. It was a stately, Old English mansion divided into seven apartments.

"It's beautiful!" she exclaimed. We had found our new home.

Judi enjoyed the social life at CRDS, found a job at

the University of Rochester, and was happy for the first few months. Johnny stayed with a woman in the downstairs apartment and did not have to leave our building for child care.

CRDS was true culture shock, however. The midsixties were turbulent, but I never expected to encounter the absolute despair that was a part of life at seminary. William Hamilton was just beginning to gain some notoriety for his teaching that, although there had once been an omnipotent, omniscient God who ruled the universe, He had died. In our time, in our existence, God is dead. People spent a lot of time trying to figure out what he meant.

Some thought he was trying to shock the church into new life. Others knew exactly what he meant. He made the comment in class that he and his school would get along tremendously well with the Reformed Jewish tradition: they had no Messiah; his school had no God. Hamilton's disciples included all kinds of students who were in rebellion against their conservative backgrounds. There was little support, however, among the faculty for Dr. Hamilton, and the students who took his teaching to heart for any length of time were a minority.

Meanwhile, the student body was out fighting the battles of social justice. Soon after my arrival on campus I turned on the TV to find some of our upper classmen chained across a major street in Rochester to protest the housing policies of local real estate brokers.

The next day, Wednesday, I went to chapel and found the place virtually deserted. On the way out a professor said to me, "No one goes to chapel here except the 'fundies.' "

The theological diet was a kind of hobo stew. Academic freedom meant essentially that everyone was on his own. We studied under liberal, neo-orthodox, and "guess me if you can" theologians. I suspect, looking back, there were one or two evangelical professors on campus, but their leanings would have had to be covered with enough sophistry that no one would recognize them.

By the time my first year at CRDS was completed, I wasn't sure where I was theologically. During a coffee break with a student whose background was very similar to mine, I said, "Jim, how's it going for you here? I know I can't go back to where I came from, and I don't like where I feel as though I'm going."

"Kind of lost, huh?" he replied.

"For sure!" I was delighted to find a kindred spirit.

We continued talking, and soon there were several of us discussing the same issue. We were all in some way going through the same experience. None of that group, except for myself, is in parish ministry today. An upper classman suggested, "When you come here and get stripped of everything you brought with you, there is no reason to be in the church—nothing to be excited about. If there's no God, then why in the world bother? These professors have their studies. They are excited about manuscripts or pieces of old pottery and stuff like that. But us? We came to learn how to proclaim the gospel. If there is no gospel or if there is no certainty about the gospel, then there is nothing to say. And if there is nothing to say then who on earth wants to be a preacher?''

My heart fired up a bit as he spoke, but I would soon dismiss that fire as nostalgia for a lost security. Dr. Hamilton had addressed the issue by talking about liberals who long to ''sneak back to camp'' and preach the gospel once more, even though they no longer accept the same tenets intellectually.

With the build-up of uncertainty came more friction and distance between Judi and me. She could not fully appreciate my intellectual and faith struggles. I thought I might be able to keep some ideas and concepts from my background and let go of others that were no longer acceptable, but I kept feeling I had grabbed the loose end of a knit sweater and *everything* was coming unraveled.

Judi's approach was too simple. ''Don't let those things trouble you. Don't believe things that upset you.''

''Terrific. 'Don't believe things that upset you.' How foolish.''

Another favorite remedy she had was, ''Just put things out of your mind that trouble you.'' She apparently could do that. I could not.

When my father called me from Timmins, Ontario, to ask if I could come and work with him for the summer in a mine, I was delighted. This would be a break from school and the mental uproar. It would give us some much needed funds for the next year, and it would be a three-month break from Judi and the growing tension between us.

Judi was pregnant again, and that brought additional tension. I should have seen the signs when she was watching those Johnson & Johnson's Baby Powder commercials.

"Oh, John, isn't he cute!" she would squeal when she watched those little babies they pick for TV.

When she told me she was pregnant I responded, "Oh, no! Why, Judi? We didn't need a baby now. I'm not even sure what I'm going to do for a career!"

That kind of talk made her anxious. A new career meant change, and her way to handle change was to put it out of her mind. During one of my attempts to discuss my struggle and my thoughts about maybe taking a different direction with my career life, she changed the subject. I yelled at her, "Ignore it, and it will go away! Right?"

"Right," she snapped as she walked away.

I really missed Judi and Johnny over the summer. We wrote several love letters to each other for the first time in our marriage. It was the only time we had ever been apart. She would tell me how sensitive Johnny was to her feelings. She continued to work all day at the university and left Johnny at the sitter's downstairs.

Judi wrote, "He seems to be able to tell that I'm just worn out, and he's so good about it. I just thank God for such a good and understanding four-year-old!"

The summer was good and getting back to my family and to school for the fall was even better. For a while.

The old struggles soon resumed, and I didn't like the

continuing feeling that there was little purpose in my being at this school. I was losing the last vestiges of my faith.

William Hamilton brought Thomas J. J. Altizer to campus for lectures on the death of God. God was about all I had left, and two other students in my class felt the same. The three of us gathered on the first evening of this "Death of God" festival and wrote a "Death of God Liturgy," which we decided to post on the bulletin board late that night when no one was looking.

"I've lost just about everything else," one of the fellows said. "If I lose God, too, I'm sunk!"

Our task was completed just after midnight. Carefully we stole through the hallways and posted our liturgy across from the central office where we knew Dr. Hamilton would come first thing in the morning.

We stood back and admired our work.

A LITURGY FOR THE DEATH OF GOD

Call to Worship

(Since there is really nothing to worship there will be no call to it.)

Hymn

"O God Our Help in Ages Past—
No Help in Years to Come"

Scripture

Dr. Altizer will read selections from Nietzsche and Kafka.

Prayer

(Since there is no longer a Divine Being to whom we may pray, the congregation will dialogue with and encounter each other and express to each other their regrets at the passing of the Lord God Almighty in our time, in our history, and in our experience.)

Sermon

(Dr. Hamilton will read a play he has written expressing the pain of life without God.)

Hymn

"The Church Has No Foundation"

Communion

There is no point in Holy Communion. However, there is a keg of beer and some pretzels in the narthex where the congregation may gather for eating, drinking, and merry-making . . . *for tomorrow we die!*

After a short night's sleep, the three of us met for early morning vigil across from the central office. Dr. Hamilton was predictable in his morning routine. He would come to collect his mail (which was heavy these days) and then read the bulletin board for the current news.

Right on schedule, he came down the hall at 7:45 A.M. He glanced at his mail and then turned to the bulletin board. His eyes suddenly fixed with intensity on our liturgy. He read with a look of disgust that increasingly turned his usually cheerful countenance into an ugly, mean scowl. He ripped his pen from his pocket and wrote something on it, looked up and down the hallway, and then stormed to his office.

We waited until we thought it was safe. Then it was a track meet to see who could get there first. When we saw Dr. Hamilton's message, we roared. He had written in broad, angry strokes:

"THIS IS BLASPHEMY!"

I took out my own pen and wrote right under his angry remark: "Against whom?"

The bulletin board was the center of attention that morning. Though several faculty members seemed quite disgusted that this should appear during the time when Dr. Altizer was a guest of Dr. Hamilton on campus, academic freedom seemed to dictate that it remain.

Inside, I was sick in spirit. I felt as though my life had no center. I was working as an intern in an American Baptist Church where I had responsibility for youth work, but the contacts there were little comfort. Church life no longer resembled what I had entered this whole process for. My own internal agitation made the relationship between Judi and myself increasingly difficult. Having committed herself to being a pastor's wife, she did not like even the slightest hint that I would not continue in that course. She stayed busy with her job and with our new son, Jaie, who came to us in December of 1965.

The weeks and months blurred into two years, and I spent another all night session with myself.

"What in God's name am I doing here? How I wish I could go back to where I came from!" I shrieked inside. I remembered the evening service at our first home church when the Holy Spirit was present so powerfully. Now I was thinking in terms of events like that being little more than mass psychological manipulation. The Holy Spirit who had been active in my conversion and call to ministry, I now saw as only an abstract projection of a psychological need. I desperately wanted to be able to once again be with the fellowship of the church that had meant so much to Judi and me. I wished a thousand times for the "joy of my salvation." Then a startling thought came to my mind with the horror of a nightmare. *I could not go back if I wanted to!*

That recognition brought a terrifying flood of doubt. My mind reviewed those things I once had held to be the joy of my life. There was almost nothing left. The Bible had become the religious history of the Jews with addendum by a Christian community. The New Testament was filled with ancient mythology. I had no desire left to reach anyone with the message that had once set my own heart on fire. There seemed to be no point in it all.

At the same time, there was no enthusiasm in my own heart for life as it now was. As the destructive flood inside me picked up power, I watched almost as a detached observer. Everything was being swept away that had ever meant anything to me. Even the few absolutes I had before I met Jesus Christ were eroding.

A final question began to emerge from within. I tried desperately to block it out. But it kept coming and coming until it exploded within my mind like dynamite.

"Please, God, *no!*"

The question came anyway. "John, do you believe in God?"

The answer came in spite of my plea that it would at least wait for a while.

"I really do not know anymore!"

With that came a shudder from the depths of my spirit and a sob from the bottom of my soul. I groaned and wept for a time, and the past few years since I had entered William Jewell College rushed through my mind. *There is absolutely no sense in being here,* I thought. *I went into the ministry because of a call. I wanted people to come to know the Jesus Christ who had made Himself known to me . . . and I don't believe that anymore. Hell, I don't even believe in a call!*

Before I went to bed that night, I stopped at the door to the boys' bedroom. I looked at Johnny's small, five-year-old form stirring gently in the night. Jaie was sleeping like a rock. "Oh, God," I whispered. "I wanted to give you kids so much. I wanted you to have a family like your mother's. I wanted you never to know the fear and emptiness that plagued me all my life."

I could taste the salt from the bitter tears that stung my lips.

"I don't know if I can live like this anymore, Johnny. I'm worse off than I was before I met your mother!"

I stopped, frightened. For the first time in my life, I thought about suicide. "Maybe I just need some sleep," I reasoned. I felt as though I had just gone ten rounds with the Devil himself as I drifted off to sleep. I wanted to pray, but there was no prayer to be found. I felt as though I wanted to reach out to the best friend I'd ever had only to remember that the friend had died.

I tried a bit of a prayer anyway. It was just one word. "Help!"

The next morning after breakfast I headed out the door in my best suit. Surprised, Judi asked, "John, where are you going?"

"To find a job," I replied.

"And when he had spent everything, a great famine arose in that country, and he began to be in want" *(Luke 15:14).*

8

Snake in the Grass

Imagine a world where there is no turmoil, struggle, or conflict; a world where there is intimate communion between God and man. In this world there is no fear, anxiety, ulcers, or Pepto Bismol. It is a beautiful paradise where every human heart would love to exist. Even the thought of this world brings a sense of peace.

The world of Adam and Eve.

There is one single question that destroyed that world: "Hath God said . . .?" It was the question of the snake in the grass. Adam and Eve gave up everything they had as that one question wound its way through the convictions they had held about what God had told them. Finally, deciding that God did not say, or should not have said, they accomplished the destruction of their lives.

Into a world of pristine beauty came blame, invective,

guilt, and shame, all because of one simple question: "Hath God said . . . ? Did God really tell you?"

I had read Harry Emerson Fosdick's autobiography, *The Living of These Days,* and could relate very easily to his own facing of that ancient question. He wrote, "Just when that first crack in the old structure began I am not sure, but it concerned the stories of the strong man, Samson. . . . I did not have to believe anything simply because it was in the Bible. . . . The old basis of authority was gone."[1]

L. Harold DeWolf's, *The Case for Theology in Liberal Perspective,* begins in chapter one with a clear statement that God hath *not* said; well, at least not really: "Strictly speaking, the Bible itself is not the pure Word of God."[2]

In my own experience and in the experience of scores of students with whom I made the theological journey, the first and most critical juncture we encountered was the issue of the Scriptures. Were the Scriptures of God or of man? In other words, if it isn't God who said, then who does say?

The answer to that question is ultimately that man himself says. Now, since man is himself the problem in the creation, how is man going to have anything ultimate to say in terms of his own salvation?

Over the past twenty years as I have lived the pain of the loss of faith and talked with so many others who have traveled the same path, I've seen this one common theme emerge almost without fail. The inexorable slide toward a loss of faith began with a surrender of the view that the

Scriptures were inspired. Sometimes it was a wholesale tossing off of the inspiration of the Bible. Most times, however, it was an inch by inch surrender. A kind of a "Yes, but . . ." approach to the question, "Hath God said?"

"Yes, the Bible is the Word of God, as it comes to us *through* the Bible. The Bible is not the Word of God, but rather the *words* of God. The Bible *contains* the word of God." All of this takes place under the guise of intellectual respectability. The rejection of the Bible as the Word of God has somehow come to be assumed as a requisite of intelligent, thinking people.

Be sure and be warned! Once you begin that surrender, however slight you may think it is, you have engaged in a process that does not end until every major foundation for faith and ministry has been destroyed. I have scores of friends who will argue that they have discovered new foundations and a new kind of faith, but with rare exceptions their churches are not ruled by Christ, and there is no desire to reach people with the gospel. The gospel with which they seek to reach people has been emptied of its power, and nothing resembling the power of new birth and holiness ever happens for them.

All of this takes place in the name of freedom. One supposedly is freed from an archaic world view, an outdated piety, and religious ignorance. Please know, however, this is no freedom at all, for it leads away from liberty in Christ, a liberty only rarely regained. The freedom expounded by so-called liberal Christianity is in reality enslavement to darkened human rationality.

Once you have been captured by the power of the Holy Scriptures after coming alive in Christ, then you already know what freedom is all about. The freedom promised by those who would have you surrender your view of Scripture as the Word of God is an empty charade. What seemed to Eve to be a harmless, simple taste of an eye-catching bit of fruit was a poison that destroyed every true freedom until the incarnation of the Lord Jesus Christ.

Thus, loss of my own sense of call began with that ancient question of the snake in the grass, "Hath God said . . . ?" That loss, along with the loss of every major belief I had once held, was the most painful vacuum of my entire life. And from that central loss came all the rest, and a wasteland of meaninglessness. To suddenly discover that I had lost the one experience that had given a true anchor and purpose to my life was utterly heartbreaking. If you are anywhere near that kind of experience, I can tell you with authority there is nothing out there to await you.

The best known and perhaps greatest evangelist of our time himself told of the time the snake in the grass came to him. In a touching magazine interview he acknowledged, "I did go through a period in the late Forties of doubting the infallibility and authority of Scripture. That was settled on my knees . . . when I accepted by faith the Bible as the authoritative and infallible Word of God."[3]

Without that step of faith, perhaps the evangelical

world would have missed one of history's greatest champions for Christ. The evangelist, of course, is Billy Graham.

I am grateful that God has enabled me to be with a few students who have struggled with this oldest of all issues. I am grateful because my message to them is simple and straightforward: "Go home! There's nothing for you in the far country." The way back home is long and painful, and not all that head that direction ever make it.

9

The Wasteland

Welcome to
NEW YORK STATE EMPLOYMENT SERVICE
Please walk in.

The sign on the door was the warmest welcome I would receive at the New York Employment Service. I entered a massive room filled with steel desks, a maze of portable metal partitions, and fifty employment counselors.

I stood before a desk behind which a small man sat looking at papers. I continued to stand in front of that desk and wondered how much practice it had taken this man to become such an expert in pretending that people weren't there.

A hand reached toward me, holding a form. "Sit down over there and fill this out, and someone will be with you shortly.'' The gruff voice emerged mysteriously, almost as a Gregorian chant, from the form at the desk. Its lips were tightly gripping a cigar. I did not see the lips move when I heard the voice.

The voice had not indicated where ''over there'' was, so I picked out a chair and sat down. With a *Sports Illustrated* magazine for support, I filled out the form.

I waited for two and a half hours and wondered just what ''shortly'' meant here at the employment service. It seemed to be wise, however, not to ask the man at the desk. The room was large and cold. The gray steel desks, brown tile, and huge drapeless windows created the feeling of a wilderness. I felt very insecure, and my eyes darted about the room hoping for a glimmer of compassion somewhere in the mass of faces. I could see nothing but irritation and boredom. The most frequent sentence that I could make out in the din of voices was, ''Sorry, but we don't seem to have anything for you.''

Fifty job counselors and fifty job seekers all talking at once made me think back to the Tower of Babel. I wondered if this was what it sounded like. The long wait was made worse because of the inner voice that troubled me.

''C'mon, John. What are you doing here? There's no happiness in this for you. You can go back now, before it's too late!''

Thoughts like that confused me. I had made what I thought was a clear, rational decision to leave the ministry. I had put this all behind. Why was this boiling up inside me now?

This was one of several times the feeling would come

over me that I should go back. Yet, I did not fully understand what "go back" even meant. It was a feeling without clear direction. Go back to where or what? Back to Colgate-Rochester? That didn't seem right. Back to the church I had come from in the first place? How? All I had was a feeling that I should go back, but I didn't know where "back" was.

"I do not understand my own actions. For I do not do what I want, but I do the very thing I hate. Wretched man that I am! . . ." wrote the apostle Paul in Romans 7:15,24. I wondered if St. Paul would understand what it was that was going on inside me. Then I was afraid that he would understand indeed! His conclusion to the whole matter was that the "law of sin" was "at war within" him (Rom. 7:23). His rescue was through Jesus Christ.

The voice within me tugged gently. "You do believe, John. In your heart you believe. In your head you have a problem, but in your heart you believe."

But why? Why this problem with my mind? It was true. I did feel that sense of desire within my heart, but with my mind I was blocking out something important. It is faith that guides the heart, and obedience that can direct the intellect. Obedience was now a foreign word to me. Having at one time given the very throne of my life to Christ, I began almost imperceptibly, but surely, to edge Him out of my heart.

Another voice interrupted the confused whirring inside, and the still small voice was quieted as I persisted in seeking a full taste of the wasteland.

"Jewell. This way please."

By the time I looked up, the man who had called my name was half-way across the room. I walked quickly to catch up. When we reached his desk, he took my dossier and the form I had filled out. He read for a time without speaking, emitting a few grunts and groans and finally a chuckle.

No one talks here, I thought.

I would have been better off if this guy hadn't talked.

"Well, well," he started.

I knew I was in for something I wouldn't like.

"I haven't had a call for a Greek major for as long as I can remember," he continued. "Why in the world would you major in Greek? Were you going to be a teacher or something?"

"Actually, I was going to be a pastor," I said. "I spent the last two years in seminary."

"Well now, I'll be a son-of-a-gun," he exclaimed. "A pastor, huh?" He laughed and slapped his knee. "Well, I have to tell you, rev'run," he emphasized with poorly disguised hostility, "I haven't had any more calls for rev'runs with Greek majors than I have for just plain Greek majors."

Our discussion, or rather, his monologue was not about my need for a job. He rattled off a long list of complaints about the church and Elmer Gantry-type clergymen. He was another in a long list of people I've encountered who were "going to be preachers." The anger building inside me was partly stricken conscience at the fact that I was joining that long list, and partly due to his ignorance. I stood up and walked out, leaving the counselor with his mountain of paper sitting in his lap.

I decided I would go to a professional job hunting service and walked into the first one I could find after leaving the state office.

What a difference! The office was plush and warm. Strains of soft music filled the room. An attractive receptionist offered me a cup of coffee, which I had barely begun to sip when she ushered me into the office of a well-dressed, executive-looking type. The whole place oozed with success. The gentleman assured me, without even looking at my dossier, "Mr. Jewell, I'm confident we can find a meaningful, challenging position for a young man of your obvious talent."

What he was going to find was a commission on my first month's salary.

I pounded the pavement for the next three weeks following up leads. "Will we get to go home and see my parents?" Judi asked. There would, of course, be no summer vacation since I hoped I would be starting a job.

After one particularly frustrating day of job hunting, I came home and blew up at Judi. I was weary of the thick silence that had greeted me each evening after my daily search for a job.

"Why don't you ask me how it's going once in a while?" I demanded.

"I can see how it's going, John. It isn't going well. Why are you doing this, anyway?" she answered. She put down the spoon she was feeding Jaie with.

"You know very well why!" I yelled. "I am leaving

seminary. I am not going back to school in the fall. Why can't you get that through your thick head?''

Tears came to her eyes. ''You were called to preach. You got out of the Air Force to study for the ministry. You were ordained. So why are you leaving? *That's* what I can't get through my head!''

''Judi, damn it, that's all over with!'' I was furious. Why couldn't she accept reality?

Judi started crying, Jaie joined her, and Johnny seized the opportunity to shove some food into Jaie's open mouth. I went for a walk to cool off and to do my own crying.

The next morning the phone rang with an appointment. I was to see the manager of an IBM subsidiary; the job sounded like something I would be interested in. I tried to hide my anxiety as I talked with the young manager.

''Actually, you're at the top limit for age in a training position like this,'' he told me.

Top limit? Twenty-seven and I'm almost over the hill? I thought to myself.

''This is a training program with managerial possibilities, and we are bringing in some people who have a well-rounded background. I see you are a Greek major. Why did you major in Greek?''

It was a good thing I liked this guy. I was able to hide my defensiveness and quipped, ''I figured if I could do well in Greek, I could learn computer languages just as well.''

When I left his office I had a job. I was elated and felt

good for the first time in a number of weeks. I had begun to wonder whether I had any cash value in the market place. I hurried home to tell Judi that I had this terrific position with an IBM subsidiary. That would make her forget her objections. There was a note on the dining room table saying she was grocery shopping.

Finally, our car pulled into the parking lot. I began telling Judi about the job almost before her foot crossed the threshold. She took her bag of groceries to the kitchen and methodically put the food away. I followed her and talked and finished my story.

Judi had nothing to say.

"Well?" I queried.

"Well, what?" She didn't share my enthusiasm.

"I got a job, that's what!" I yelled. "It's a terrific job. It's an IBM company and that makes it a *great* job. So like I said . . . isn't that great!"

I could hardly hear her half-whispered reply as she walked out of the kitchen without even looking at me. "If you say so, John."

I exploded. Judi received the brunt of my anger and the pain that simmered within.

With all of the yelling I was doing, Johnny began a crying duet with Jaie. Judi turned and said, "I'm going to lie down," and walked off into our bedroom.

Judi always was an expert at letting me stew. She can lie down and take a nap with an emotional freight train going through the house. I need to get things ironed out immediately. She's a master at letting me hang all day Sunday, for instance, waiting for some kind of a response about my sermon. She can get me to take her out to lunch, hang up my clothes, and even unball my socks . . . all just to hear her comment about the morning's message! She especially hooked me this time.

"You're the one who didn't want me to be a preacher in the first place!" I hollered into the bedroom. I slammed the door and walked out of our place with my Interpreter's Bible packed in a box. I also had the door-knob in my hand. I would fix it tomorrow.

I took the box of books to a fellow student across the street and sold him the set for twenty-five dollars. I reasoned I would not have any more use for the set, and I was also helping a poor seminarian. Personally, I was about to become a well-to-do employee of IBM.

We moved out of the seminary housing and into a two-bedroom apartment in a large complex in Rochester. Within a few months I had thrown myself completely into the training program and was doing very well. A supervisor wrote for my first work review that he expected to be working for me in five years. I traveled to computer schools in New York City and San Francisco, where the night life received as much attention as our school. I erected a barricade around my conscience and had absolutely nothing to do with church.

Judi complained to me that she wanted to go to church and that she wanted the boys in Sunday school. I had no time for that myself, I told her, but it was fine with me if she wanted to take them. My life was absorbed by work and the social scene of the company. The only spiritual thought that ever crossed my mind was a vague twinge whenever I would by chance hear an old hymn. Beyond that feeling, I would not allow my thoughts to go.

Judi and I lived with an uneasy truce when it came to anything spiritual. We had some good times and continued to see some of our friends from the seminary, but we didn't discuss any issues having to do with church or faith. And we grew apart.

During one period of my training, I was working at night, and Judi was still working at the university during the day. We didn't see each other very much. She was in bed when I got home from work, and I was at work when she arrived home in the evening. It was difficult to come home to a quiet apartment where everyone was sleeping. I couldn't unwind, so I began to accept the invitation of some guys to join them at a local tavern where we played poker, told stories, and relaxed after the evening's work. As I listened to some of the stories about the extracurricular activity that was going on, I wondered if this was Peyton Place.

Am I capable of cheating on Judi? I wondered. I didn't think so, but things weren't going so well and there was a big fight one night after work when I came home at 3:00 A.M. after "unwinding." I started to pack, but we decided that I would at least not leave until the next day. I never did pack the suitcase, but we were in a kind of relational limbo. I never did cheat on her. Somehow, by the grace of God, I was kept from that.

Judi was worried about our marriage. She said to me with tears in her eyes during one of our arguments, "I stand at that window every night 'til at least one o'clock in the morning, wondering if you'll come home after work. I think about where you are and wonder who you are with. John, I feel so lonely.''

It had been about ten months now since I had gone to work for IBM, and an old restlessness was kicking up its heels inside. I didn't like that. I didn't want any more change in plans or in my future.

One night my career goals, which included my plan to one day be running the company, again were shaken. We had adjourned to one of the guy's homes for our winding down. That term was getting to be a joke; we talked about changing it to winding "up."

We were laughing and telling stories, and I took my turn at telling a rousing good story about the priest, minister, and rabbi. We had a good laugh and one of the guys said to me, "You know, Jewell, you're a heluva guy! When I first heard that you had been a preacher, I thought you'd be a real stick in the mud. But you know what? You're a lotta fun!" He slapped my back, knocked me over with his breath, and slurred on about something a preacher he had known in his youth had done to make his family mad and they never went back to church again.

The whole evening faded into the background. The guys were still playing cards and laughing, but I didn't hear another word. My mind was turning his comment over and over. "You're a lotta fun."

Fun. A lot of fun. Where had I heard that before? At one time my life had been given over totally to the pursuit of fun, and here I was again. I don't know whether I had considered myself smarter or better or different from these guys, but suddenly I was faced with the fact that I was back where I started this whole journey, the night I met Judi in the Enlisted Men's Club. Having fun!

What had this guy said? It was very plain to me that he was saying, "Jewell, you may have been a preacher, but as far as I can tell there isn't an ounce of difference between you and anyone else out here in the world!"

The party went on, but my thoughts turned back to a time when I was heartbroken for people like this. Their lives and families and marriages were in deep trouble, and there was a silent panic that brewed just beneath the surface. Many of us were on the fast track, and success was the order of the day. The material accumulation of the group I hung around with could easily have outfitted a vacation resort. Quietly beneath the facade of the "eat, drink, and be merry" game was a conspiracy called "Do not name that tune." The name of the tune was "Something very important is missing here somewhere."

In a hundred different ways it had been said, "This man knows Him" or "Certainly this fellow was with Him" for he was a minister. But my life and my actions said very loudly and clearly, "Man, I do not know what you're talking about!"

Now the cock crowed. "Jewell, you're a heluva guy!"

I drove home in a fog that night and when I parked the car, I just sat there, almost unable to go into the apartment. I was sick. Sick from the beer and sick from the same old conversations and sick of myself. I felt trapped.

The joy that had once been the foundation of my life

was totally gone. Yet, here I was on the threshold of a knowledge explosion that would make people in my new profession in fantastic demand over the next two decades. Judi and the boys would be able to have all the things I ever dreamed of. And somehow as I looked out at the future, all I could see was a vast wasteland.

I sat in that car and wept bitterly, partly for the things I had done, but mostly for the things I hadn't done. I desperately wished for the old sense of peace and fulfillment.

I wondered once again whether I wanted to live without that.

"So he went and joined himself to one of the citizens of that country, who sent him into his fields to feed swine" (Luke 15:15).

10

The Fire in My Bones

The next morning came on the heels of what seemed like only a few moments of sleep. I hoped that somehow the feelings of the previous night would pass, and it would be back to business as usual with my very promising career.

But the feeling would not go away. From that moment on, the restlessness inside me would not subside. I could no longer keep thoughts about the sorry state of my emotional and spiritual life from my mind.

The boys were playing in their bedroom one morning, and I stopped to watch them on my way to the bathroom to get the aspirin bottle. I had a raging hangover, and as I listened to their voices, I suddenly realized, "What I'm living is certainly not what I want for them."

We began looking at houses in hopes of buying our own after all these years, and that in itself made Judi much happier.

"Maybe things will be okay," she said to me one afternoon as we went to look at another house. "We'll have a home of our own finally, and we can find a church where we can go together. Things will be okay." She has the tenacity of a bulldog.

Where in the world does she get this church stuff? I thought. *Who said anything about a church?*

As we drove, I felt sorry for Judi being married to me. She was just beginning to settle into what was going on and to accept the fact that I was not going to be in pastoral ministry. I was beginning to be unsettled with what was going on and to accept the fact that I wouldn't be happy outside of pastoral ministry. It had been almost a year since we left Colgate-Rochester; just about the length of time it took Judi to adjust to a major change.

I tried, however. I tried for a season longer to keep the feeling inside down to a dull roar. A few more Rolaids to stop the burning in my stomach might help.

One of our senior programmers left the company, and I was given responsibility for one of our largest accounts. The immediate future promised tremendous economic rewards, if I could just hang in there for a while longer.

The account was a bookkeeping system for a large stockbroker. Accurate and exact daily reporting was crucial for the broker, and that was the purpose of our program for him. Even an hour's delay in our daily computer run was a serious problem.

We had just installed the new IBM 360 and had encountered several difficulites in changeover from the old

1400 series computers. The difference in capabilities could be compared to the difference between propeller-driven and jet aircraft.

One evening a critical problem developed with the program, and everything ground to a halt. An hour went by. One of my colleagues stopped to help. Two hours passed, and there was a mob around the computer examining every detail of what was going on. Soon we were joined by the manager of our office. No one could figure out what was wrong. I was on the phone to sister offices all over the country. Nothing seemed to work. The manager paced the floor as I watched the program "blow" for a second and a third time.

Along with the manager, a few of the other guys adjourned to a nearby tavern where they were going to try to think of something.

"Call me when you find the problem," the manager said as he walked out the door. The look on his face said, "You'd better get it figured out!"

Two more hectic hours went by, and I was able to mask the immediate problem in order to process the daily work. The manager was ecstatic that the work was done, but I knew the evening's solution was only a bandage on a serious wound.

The remainder of that night was a turning point in my life. It calls to my mind the promise of God in Jeremiah: "The people who survived the sword found grace in the wilderness . . ." (31:2).

What happened next was indeed "grace in the wilderness."

When I went to bed that night, sleep overtook me so fast I was unconscious before my head hit the pillow. I was living on coffee, cigarettes, and Pepto Bismol-Rolaid cocktails. My mind would not disengage from the problem with our computer program even in sleep.

I can recall as clearly now as the moment it happened. I saw two IBM punched cards in a dream. The computer instructions on the cards were the answer to the problem with the stock broker's program. The color of the cards and the printing were clear.

I woke up with a start. It was 3:30 A.M. I got up and dressed in the dark, fumbling around and knocking something off the dresser.

"What are you doing?" Judi mumbled in a half-awake voice.

"I'm going into the office. I think I've found the answer to a problem that could cost us one of our largest accounts," I replied as I made my way to the front door.

Judi's sleepy call pleaded with me as I left the house, "John, you're going crazy. *It's 3:30 in the morning!*"

My race to the office was undertaken with the hope that the traffic officers would all be on coffee break or dozing in their squad cars. When I got to the office, I quickly punched up the two cards I had seen in my dream and entered the new data with the day's work. There was a long, slow sorting process which was done by magnetic tape. I had to wait for that tape sort before the rest of the program would be completed.

With coffee, cigarette, and aching stomach, I alternately stood and then sat while watching the tape drives churn away.

"Lord, please let this thing work!" I still had my emergency prayers on file for ready use. I hoped this prayer would be heard, much as the driver of a car with a flat tire hopes the spare tire has air in it.

With all of its auxiliary equipment, central processing center, and blinking lights, the 360 seemed like a giant electromechanical brain. The large room with blinking lights and the hum of the machines created a surrealistic feeling. I had never been here alone like this. I felt a presence. I almost wanted to ask, "Who is it? Is it You, Lord?" I was half afraid that if I did ask, I would get an answer. I was anxious, tired, and a feeling of numbness came over me.

"Maybe Judi's right. Maybe I am going nuts!"

I don't know why, but several people came to mind whom I hadn't thought about for some time.

There was Jack from William Jewell College. Jack was a Captain in the Salvation Army. He was struggling with his faith and with the challenge that the Bible was not God's inspired Word. He was in my New Testament class, and we would occasionally share our reactions to the day's "de-mythologizing." One day after the historical reality of the resurrection was questioned, Jack said, "If I don't leave this place, I'm going to end up leaving the ministry."

I heard later that Jack became manager of a grocery store.

Then there was George. George was originally from an Assembly of God background and was going to go to graduate school after seminary to get another degree so he could teach sociology. "Do you ever think about going back to pulpit ministry?" I asked him.

"Yes," he said, "I sometimes get a real urge to go back to where I came from, but it's like getting kicked out of the Garden. You can never go back once you've eaten the fruit of that forbidden tree."

I thought of Mike. Mike was with one of our offices on the West Coast. Every time Mike would have a couple of drinks, he would find me and ask, "Did I ever tell you that I was going to be a minister?"

"Yes, Mike, you've told me that," I would reply in vain. Mike would go ahead and tell me about his beginnings in a Baptist church. He had attended college and seminary in the Southern Baptist system. I was uncomfortable as I thought about him now, because he described for me a process that began with doubts about the reliability of the Bible and ended up with a loss of faith. He had also lost his personal value system and moral framework. A crisis in his ministry was finally forced by an extramarital affair.

Oh, and Don. Don's story was a winner. He plainly said that he had never experienced a call and that he was never really sure what he had believed about Christ in the first place. He remarked to me just before he graduated from seminary, "Here I am, about to receive a Master of Divinity degree, and I can't quote three verses from the Bible."

The 360 continued to blink and hum. I was starting to shake inside, and the feeling turned to panic. I wanted to run and keep on running. Perhaps I was afraid the program wasn't going to work.

"No, that's not it!" I said out loud. The problem was the way I was thinking and living. That blasted inner emptiness was starting all over again.

"What am I doing here?" I complained to that 360. It didn't care. It just blinked and hummed. I decided I didn't want to spend my life relating to machines—even machines that cost millions of dollars.

A flashing red light appeared on the console of the 360. The tape sort was finished. All I had to do was to push one last button, and I would know whether this middle of the night trip had been worth it.

My finger was visibly shaking as I reached out to push the button that would start the printing of the stock reports. I took a deep breath, closed my eyes, and pushed. I'm almost convinced that I could measure the millisecond that it took for that printer to start.

It worked! A flood of relief and pride brought a bit of life to my tired, aching body and lifted for a few moments my terrific sense of foreboding. This would be tremendous for my standing. Hard work and success were well rewarded. Mistakes brought swift shuffling off to the back rooms of the company. I was definitely on the fast track! I was going to be one of the company's whiz kids.

I couldn't wait to go home and tell Judi about this brilliant feat. On second thought, I could wait. The euphoria died quickly as it dawned on me that Judi couldn't care less about what I was doing with machines in the middle of the night.

I went, instead, to an all night restaurant, drank more coffee, smoked more cigarettes, and reflected.

"Why did I wake up? Is it possible . . . even remotely possible . . . that the Lord wanted to get me out of bed in the middle of the night?" I knew then for certain that I did not want a career in data processing. I could climb that ladder of success if I chose to, but the idea suddenly seemed very empty to me.

I drove back to the office and left a note on my supervisor's desk.

Program works! I'm dead. Won't be in today. It is today already. Jewell—7:30 A.M.

Three hours of sleep brought a bit of relief to my aching body. I called the dean of the seminary and asked if I could see him. I hadn't talked with him for a year. He was gracious and open to my coming in that afternoon to talk with him about finishing the requirements for graduation.

As I walked the hallways of the school once again, I felt a strange sensation. There was a tremendous sense of relief that accompanied my decision to leave IBM. It was as though a thousand pounds was lifted from my soul.

I am firm in my conviction that what happened next was God's way of saying yes to that thought.

I glanced down the hall, and my eyes were riveted to

the eyes of a young black preacher who had been a classmate. A mile-wide smile crossed his face, and a light jumped from his eyes as he ran toward me laughing and shouting, "If I say, 'I will not mention him, or speak any more in his name,' there is in my heart as it were a burning fire shut up in my bones, and I am weary with holding it in, and I cannot" (Jer. 20:9).

What happened inside me as he spoke those words is something I can not describe to this day, but I can feel it. Tears filled my eyes. The very closest thing I can think of to describe what happened inside me is the passage of Scripture in Luke 1 which describes Elizabeth's reaction to Mary's visit. ". . . The babe leaped in her womb and Elizabeth was filled with the Holy Spirit" (v. 41). When Steven spoke those words of Jeremiah to me, something inside leaped for joy. Something that came from beyond me, for that kind of joy had faded in my life as though it had been buried in some kind of spiritual amnesia. His words have never left my heart: "Fire in my bones!"

"When he came to himself he said, 'How many of my father's hired servants have bread and enough to spare, but I perish with hunger! I will arise and go to my father . . ." (Luke 15:17,18).

11

The Maze

"The death of God means that, although there was once an omnipotent, omniscient God, there is now no such God. He has in reality died."

William Hamilton was responding to a student who had asked for the specific meaning of the "death of God."

Terrific start to my new beginning I thought to myself. It was my first class on the first day of my coming back to seminary to finish my degree.

The experience of "fire in my bones" was a real event. There was no way I could deny the fact that something powerful had taken place. Something compelling stirred within. I could feel the meaning of St. Paul saying, ". . . For necessity is laid upon me. Woe to me if I do not preach the gospel!" (1 Cor. 9:16).

I was, nevertheless, in a difficult and vulnerable place. I felt as though I were in the jaws of a vice. I felt compelled to preach, but I honestly did not know what I would preach about. I was open, searching, and in desperate need of spiritual guidance at this precarious time in my life.

My heart was in the right place, but my mind was lagging behind somewhere. I felt like a spiritual schizophrenic. If I had followed the impulse of my inner emotional state, I would gladly have returned to my home church. The difficulty with that, however, was that I might as well have been a million miles away from where I was when I began my journey with Christ. Although my heart was full with a longing to go home, my intellect could not—or would not—cooperate.

A psalm came to mind as I sat half listening to Dr. Hamilton continue his lecture.

> *By the waters of Babylon, there we sat down and*
> *wept,*
> *when we remembered Zion.*
> *How shall we sing the LORD's song*
> *in a foreign land?'' (Ps. 137:1,4).*

I could feel the words. I knew the pain that came from desperately missing the Father's home. My Babylonian captor was the rationalism that rules the theological throne of contemporary liberalism.

Judi did ask me, "How was it?" when I came home to our apartment that evening.

"Okay," I answered, "Hamilton is still preaching his atheism, and the students are pretty much committed to saving the world through social activism. Not much is new."

"You're sure that this is what you want though, huh?" There was so much hope and longing for stability in Judi's tone. "I mean, John, this is *it,* isn't it? You are going to be a pastor—right?"

I was uncomfortable. "Yes, Judi," I hedged, "But please don't bug me!"

"I'm not bugging you," she responded, "I just want to be sure. I know a lot of wives who have to go through the experience of becoming a preacher's wife once, but no one I know of has done it twice!"

I laughed in spite of myself. "I'm going to the library tonight. I have some work to do, and I need some time to be alone and think."

I sat in the library and tried to think through just where I was theologically. My view of Jesus Christ was conditioned heavily by liberal theology. I had accepted a college professor's explanation that "God was focused as much in Jesus as He can be focused in any person . . . and that person remain a human being." Jesus' death on the cross opened up a way of love for us, but I could not make intellectual sense out of the idea of substitutionary atonement. The Scriptures were sacred history and as such very important.

This did not qualify me for a return to the church I had begun my ministry in. *So where do I go?* I thought.

I entered a maze.

I did not want to be where I was.

I did not know where I wanted to go.

There is one critical thread that runs through the whole maze. Paul Tillich was a big part of my study in those last months at seminary. In his *Systematic Theology,* he wrote, "More than two centuries of theological work have been determined by the apologetic problem. The Christian message and the modern mind has been the dominating theme since the end of classical orthodoxy. The perennial question has been: Can the Christian message be adapted to the modern mind without losing its essential and unique character?"[1]

This concept of the modern mind was the thread I could trace from the beginnings of my slide toward apostasy right up to my present state. Throughout my whole educational development, I had listened to professors daily hammer away at the reality of the supernatural because of its offence to the modern mind. My own commitment to rationalism as the supreme function had gained for me nothing but the complete loss of purpose in ministry.

There are two possible ways to perceive the modern mind. On the one hand, the modern mind is the child of the enlightenment, free from the irrelevance and superstition of the supernatural. From the perspective of what St. Paul calls the "natural" man, the modern mind has faith that man's intellectual and rational capacity can ultimately redeem him.

On the other hand, one can realize that the human intellect is unredeemed and therefore unable to perceive the simplicity of the gospel.

I glanced up at the library clock when I noticed that students were leaving. I was not finished. I still needed some time alone, so I drove to a favorite spot on Lake Ontario and went to sit on the beach. The waves were gently rolling to the shore, and my heart was almost pleading with God to give me my old faith back. Sitting there by the lake reminded me of how St. Peter's response to Christ on the Galilean shore had once created a fire within me.

"What's my purpose?" I had the sense of call, but what in the world was the purpose of it? I once had a broken heart for people who were bewildered and lost; separated from the love of God. I cared not whether I achieved a single thing if God would only be pleased to bring men and women home to Himself through the message He had placed within me . . . if He would only "seek and save the lost" through the love that had so utterly changed my life.

I wanted that to be my purpose again. I wept and pounded the sand because it was not my purpose. The human intellect—the modern mind—undid the whole pupose of ministry with a single question: "Would a loving, kind God really allow anyone to be eternally lost? Now that wouldn't make sense, would it?"

The collapse of the essential purpose of the church was apparent in a popular paperback book edited by Stephen Rose called *Who's Killing the Church?* The book was a loosely organized collection of essays all saying in one form or another that the church was meaningless and irrelevant to the modern world. In an article that Rose himself penned, the suggestion was made that modern man has outgrown the gospel message. Rose was scornful of an article from a popular Christian magazine because of a statement it contained: "The question of the Philippian jailor still takes priority today: 'Sirs, what must I do to be saved?' " Mr. Rose then berated the magazine for suggesting that, "Paul's answer should be the message of the church in this sophisticated nuclear age: 'Believe on the Lord Jesus Christ and thou shalt be saved.' "[2]

As I sat by the lake that night, I knew at the depths of my being that my purpose for being in the ministry was no longer the calling of individuals to repentance and faith in Jesus Christ. I remembered very clearly my home church pastor saying, "It would be better to be as ignorant as a hog than to be a liberal!" The way I was feeling right at that moment, I would have been willing to become ignorant if I could have received back my purpose.

"It's like Adam and Eve trying to pretend they weren't naked. Once they recognized their naked state and lost their innocence, there was no turning back," I thought out loud.

I went home that night unsure as to where I was going in my ministry. I was definitely a theological liberal whose liberalism was turning up bankrupt, and there was nothing to take its place.

The next few years would find my ministry at the

mercy of my frenzied search for purpose. Sometimes it would be in the form of a commitment to the social gospel, sometimes searching for peace of mind in the encounter group movement. And most of the time there would be nothing but a great black void.

A small United Church of Christ was seeking a steady pulpit supply, and I was contacted about filling their vacancy just before I graduated from Colgate-Rochester. The remuneration included the use of a parsonage; Judi would be able to keep her job at the University of Rochester. I was delighted to accept the call.

During the first two or three months, things went very well at the church. I dipped into my sermon barrel and pulled out some of the more popular messages. Attendance improved, and there was a bit of excitement in the air. A task force for study and renewal was created and we explored, studied, and searched for the meaning of being God's people in the modern world. We read *Who's Killing the Church?* and other renewal literature, which complained about God's people and berated them for not having created a better world.

My own lack of purpose and inner emptiness caught up with me, and I began to feed the congregation out of my own emptiness. There was, in a very strange way, a certain honesty and consistency in Dr. Hamilton's "death of God" theology. Hamilton and Altizer wrote in the preface to their book, *The Death of God,*

Radical theology is peculiarly a product of the mid-twentieth century; it has been initiated by Barth and neo-orthodoxy into a form of theology which can exist in the midst of the collapse of Christendom and the advent of secular atheism. It has also learned from Paul Tillich and Rudolph Bultmann the necessity for theology to engage in a living dialogue with the actual world and history which theology confronts.[3]

The book's dedicatory page says simply, "In memory of Paul Tillich."

Hamilton's conception of his god's death was accurate in that it was the very logical conclusion to the whole liberal mentality. It is the end of the thread that begins with the false assumption that something called the "modern mind" requires abandonment of the supernatural. Hamilton, as it turns out, may have been the *least* dangerous of all the professors I had in seminary. He may deserve a second look; at least he knew he was without God.

In any case, Hamilton's theological position was my spiritual condition. I had a pulpit, but no real message. Thus, it was probably as much the Lord's idea as my own that I accept a call to a church in Rockford, Illinois, as an associate pastor for youth work and education. At least I was not in a pulpit. There was a sign at the end of this part of the maze: Dead End.

12

The Jonah Factor

One major excitement in our move to Rockford was the opportunity to buy our own home. I had G.I. Bill benefits, which enabled us to secure a mortgage. Judi was thrilled about a small, gray Cape Cod that sat on a quiet street near the school Johnny would attend. The house was about forty years old and had abundant charm: sculptured trim, white picket fence, and a fruit cellar off the basement.

The day we moved in, Johnny went around the neighborhood knocking on every door saying, "Hi! I'm Johnny Jewell, and I just moved into the gray house down the street. Do you have any kids my age I can play with?" He never knew a stranger, Wilma Wolf had said. He came running through the front door very excited about his discoveries. "Guess what? I found two friends and a girl!"

Two weeks after we moved in, Judi found a secretarial job with a local electric company. She had to work because the house brought additional bills, and my salary would not adequately support us. I watched her one morning getting Johnny ready for school, Jaie ready for the baby sitter, and herself ready for work. I helped with the driving, the lunch fixing, or whatever else would expedite the rushed morning routine, but this day I was struck by how hard Judi had worked all during our marriage. She had worked outside the home almost since the day we were married, except for a couple of weeks after Johnny was born and a couple of months when we had the house on the hill behind the church in Kansas City. She was working hard so that we would get ahead. I was working hard emotionally, feeling lost whenever I stopped to take account of myself.

I spent the majority of my first year in Rockford majoring in social action. I organized and directed the grape boycott and became intensely involved with the Viet Nam peace movement. I followed Jesus the social prophet, the liberator, the radical. Stephen Rose wrote, "If there is any graspable image of Jesus in our time it begins with the fact that he was an agitator."[1] I think I liked that image because it was so easy to project my own inner agitation onto the world around me; my agitation was "righteous agitation" over the collective sin of the social order.

Social, corporate sin was the real culprit in the world,

said Rose. The church should address the sin of the multinational corporations, the immorality of war, and the oppression of institutional racism, instead of concerning itself with the petty sins of individuals. The Bible itself was seen as providing the marching orders for social activists. "The Bible is a book about agitators . . . Biblical agitation—the passion of the prophets for loyalty to God and for the evidence of that loyalty in human relations—is a more worthwhile subject to study, than, for example, Biblical moralism which hardly exists in the Bible,"[2] Rose affirmed.

Spiritually, I was on sabbatical. Personal piety, morality, or sin was not the issue for modern Christians. The only prayers I prayed were pastoral prayers during worship, invocations at various community gatherings, and grace at mealtimes in our home. I was empty inside, but I kept so busy outwardly that there was no time to face the inner darkness. I was attending meetings and strategy sessions at least five nights out of the week. Two afternoons a week and Saturday mornings were given to picketing a popular local grocery chain. Judi marched with me at times, and Johnny became the youngest picket in Rockford. He was learning social justice at what I thought was a marvelous time of his life. He wouldn't have the prejudice or bondage to materialism that had infected most of our society, I promised myself.

A call came from the principal of Johnny's school one day saying he had gotten angry at his teacher and had run out of the building. "He came back and apologized though, Reverend Jewell, and I think everything is okay now. But I just wanted you to know that sometimes John has trouble with his teacher."

I didn't think this too serious for a third grade child and passed it off as an isolated incident. He was doing a lot of learning in other ways from my involvements.

In spite of working very hard to heal the wounds and fractures of the world, I was fractured and wounded inside. Victories here and there in the grape boycott, raising twenty-eight thousand dollars through a city-wide march for hunger, and marching for peace in Viet Nam did nothing to fill the void that was demanding attention inside.

I attended frequent cocktail parties for people in the "movement." One brought my activity to a screeching halt. This particular assembly was the largest collection of hippies, union agitators, nuns, political activists, and other avant garde types I had ever seen. It was a raucous gathering.

I was sipping on a cocktail talking with a fellow who had resigned his priesthood, making an observation about Jesus being a person committed to liberation of oppressed peoples. His response stopped me cold. He quoted some writer who I assumed reflected his own feelings, to the effect that, "Jesus was a bastard and got everything he deserved."

A shock went through me. It was as though I was hearing Satan himself. Job's wife had suggested that Job "Curse God, and die" (Job 2:9). I had tossed off every vestige of superstition and supernatural gibberish, but with this remark, I waited for a second to see if the guy would draw another breath. It was the end of the evening for me. I stepped into a corner and suddenly felt like a stranger in that crowd. I looked around the room, and it was as though the "scales" that St. Paul spoke of fell from my eyes.

This was a group of mixed up, troubled people (not the least of whom was me), who sought peace desperately in the world because there was none in their lives. Our real problem was not the war in Viet Nam, but the war inside. As I listened to the rhetoric, I was pained by the superficiality of what I had become. Beyond the shock of what I could see in myself, I was surprised. Whatever else had become of my relationship with Jesus Christ, I could not bear the epithet this angry, ex-priest had pronounced upon the Name I had once loved so passionately.

I felt like Jonah. I was running from God and from the message He had once given to me. I felt as though I was on shaky ground, on a stormy sea, and I thought briefly that I just might be truly disturbed. I let that thought go, however, because I had a feeling I *was* disturbed. The spiritual disturbance was as serious—perhaps more serious—than any emotional disturbance I could imagine. My whole liberal mentality and theology was crumbling away. On the way home from that party, I had Jonah's prayer on my lips; "When my soul fainted within me, I remembered the LORD and my prayer came to thee . . ." (Jon. 2:7).

I began to back away from my heavy involvement in the social issues that had taken so much of my time. I felt some guilt that the church had not really received what they had a right to expect from me. I turned my attention more toward my ministry in education and youth work in the church.

Another surprise was waiting for me. It came from an unlikely source. I had agreed to attend a youth camp for high school young people. I was to be a resource person for the college age young people who served as counselors for the camp. The camp counselors and three of us who were pastors met evenings after supper to discuss the day's activities, plan for the next day, and brainstorm about new ways to make Christianity "relevant" for our young people.

By and large, our approach was to allow the life-style, culture, and even whims of the high school kids to spell out the agenda for our programming. One exercise, for instance, found a small group of Beatle fans brainstorming with the question, "What do the Beatles sing about that reminds you of the things Jesus said?" The young college student who was leading the session commented that when she was in high school, John Lennon had said, "We're more popular than Jesus now." He had predicted that Christianity would vanish from the face of the earth.

That evening after supper, the staff was leaving our table when this particular girl asked me, "Do you believe in God?"

"Well, of course I believe in God," I said, "I'm a pastor." I continued to tell her about God in terms of ultimate concern and the ground of being—Tillich's language. I assumed, of course, that a bright young college girl would want to hear about faith in more sophisticated terms. I was right in line with Stephen Rose who felt that responding to people with the old-time, "Believe on the Lord Jesus Christ and thou shalt be saved" was utterly absurd in this modern age, especially with bright, modern college students.

"Don't give me all that garbage," she said. "I just want to know about your faith; I can't make any sense out of the whole thing for my own life."

What happened next surprised me even as I spoke. Without the props of sophisticated religious language or significant quotes from the latest theological journals, I was on my own. This girl wanted to hear my story, not the musings of others.

"No sermon, please," she said. "Just what you believe."

I sighed deeply and reached back to my beginnings. "Well, I came to a time when I found my life empty and without very much meaning. I tried the party life and crammed in all the good times I could as a G.I., but that all turned up empty, too. I wondered what life was all about, why in the world I was here in the first place. I met my wife about then; we were both pretty wild, I guess, but even when I was dating her, I felt burned out inside and really wanted something I could pin my life on. I needed a place to stand that would be on firm ground. It was like I was trying to balance myself standing in a rubber raft on a stormy lake with nothing to hold on to."

She laughed and nodded her head, "Yeah, I know. Go on . . . so then what?"

"My girl's parents had something that I really wanted. Judi—that's my wife—started to change, too. Her family seemed to know Jesus as though He were for real. It wasn't Religion 101 type knowing, but real knowing. I became convinced through them that Christ was honestly a part of their lives. They were happy, and their lives seemed to work. In spite of all the kicks I was out for, I wasn't happy deep inside. They seemed to have that happiness.

"I was churning inside whenever I was with them. I never thought of myself as a pious or religious person, but I really wanted to know Jesus like they knew Him. Judi's mom helped me one night by asking if I wanted to ask Jesus to enter my life and give me the kind of joy they had found in Him.

"It may sound kind of crazy, but I found myself on my knees right there in their living room, asking Jesus Christ to come into my life, to forgive me of all the wrong in my life, and to give me His gift of eternal life. That made it real! Something happened for me that I can't fully explain except to say that when Christ comes into a life He really, truly, is there changing you for the rest of your life.

"If Christ is alive and real like the New Testament says He is, then you can know Him like you know other living people. I would say I know you because I've met you. It's like that with Jesus. You can meet Him. Get introduced to Him, and He will become real for you."

I was amazed at what was happening! When forced to be genuine, I found myself telling the story of what had happened to me so many years before. As I told her what had happened to me in my encounter with Jesus Christ, my heart was aglow for a time. I was amazed at what I was saying and amazed at what was happening before my eyes.

This girl had come to camp with a downcast look about her. She had seemed lifeless and depressed at the beginning of the week-long camp. Now I watched her whole countenance change. It was one of the two or three times in my life that I witnessed a deepseated, inner change take place in a person in a matter of moments—a miracle of transformation. It was not me, or my ability to tell the story, but the Holy Spirit that took my words and did something in her life that was visibly apparent. There was, I am convinced, a complete reconstruction of her personality that was begun in that moment.

Her face was now alive with a newness. "I'm going to do that," she said. "When I go to my room, I am going to ask Him to do that for me! I never really knew He was alive before."

The next morning her roommate said to me, "I don't know what you told Jan last night, but she is not the same person who came to camp with me last week!"

I was rather startled by the whole experience. I had not even thought through what I was saying to her; the words just poured out. That episode was my first genuine encounter with a transcendent, supernatural spiritual reality since I had entered William Jewell College. It was a ministry of the Holy Spirit to both of us, to the student and to me.

The reality of that camp experience brought home another truth: I was not going to be happy outside a pulpit ministry.

I went to the senior pastor of our church and told him I was missing the pulpit and I would have to search for a place where I would have a pulpit ministry as a major part of my task. He affirmed my decision by saying, "I've only heard you a couple of times, John, but the idea makes sense to me. You do have a gift for preaching, which you should probably be using."

During the time I was talking with pulpit committees, I was spending a lot of time with the adult education program of the church. There were a few people who became very important at this stage of my journey, as I was leaving a humanistic liberalism that had fallen apart and searching out how to rebuild my faith.

Red and Barbara were one couple with whom Judi and I spent a great deal of time. They had both come from the East where they were raised in classically liberal churches. They had, however, discovered Jesus Christ as their Lord and Master, and we shared something of the devastating emptiness of that brand of church life that is devoid of the living Christ. During our last months in Rockford, the "fire in my bones" which had surfaced once again in my life longed for expression.

I felt so close to what it was that my life was all about, yet so far from what it was that I was called to be.

Shortly before we left Rockford, a social worker with whom we had placed a request for the adoption of a daughter called. I was absolutely taken by surprise. She had discouraged our request because adoptions were taking so long. "It could be a long time," she had cautioned us.

With Johnny and Jaie, we had nine months of preparation. With this little girl, Joyce, there was a two-hour wait. We went to see her that very afternoon in the foster home where she had been placed, and we brought her home. Joyce celebrated her first birthday with us two days later. What a way to have a baby!

Joyce barely felt at home when it was time to move—again. "Will we ever settle down?" Judi asked.

"Will I ever get my act together?" was all I could answer.

13

Just Before Dawn

A period of tremendous personal excitement followed my call to the pulpit of a four-hundred-member United Church of Christ in suburban Chicago. My ministry began there on Easter Sunday in 1971. In my first sermon, I said, "The resurrection means that the living Christ offers us the chance for a new beginning. If you dig into the recesses of your being, isn't this what we all long for? A new start . . . a chance to discover new meaning and new purpose for our living?"

This need for a new beginning was a cry from the depths of my own spirit. A new beginning! I longed for a new beginning.

For two years, it seemed as though that new beginning had come. Attendance at the church grew, and the members were excited about apparent signs of new life.

Judi wanted to have her own involvement in reaching out. "I want to do something to express my own Christian faith," she said. We became foster parents and began taking teen-aged girls in crisis into our home. Judi spent many nights sitting with these girls, sometimes until dawn. On occasions it meant holding their hand or taking them into her arms as the first loving person to ever hold them. At other times it meant going to school with them or showing them simple things like how to set a table for dinner.

We had four foster girls over a period of a few years. Maggie was with us from the time she was fourteen until, at twenty-two, she moved to an apartment of her own.

I had begun a Doctor of Ministry program through San Francisco Theological Seminary. My focus was church renewal. I wanted to study everything I could and then come up with *the* program. I hoped to create a program of renewal that would finally bring the power and joy of the early church to our church.

There was one fatal flaw in my scheme. Everything in this reconstruction was centered on the word "I." *I* was going to create a renewal program. *I* was building my faith all over again. The power and the drive for the journey home was something *I* undertook on my own. It was the most dangerous and critical time of the whole journey—and the prelude to the darkest hour of my life.

In his second letter to Timothy, St. Paul warns of the perilous times of the last days. A part of that warning has to do with those "having a form of godliness, but denying the power thereof" (2 Tim. 3:5 KJV).

Though I had experienced a longing for a return of my lost faith in Christ, the power was not there. Just over ten years earlier, I had given myself to Christ unreservedly. Two years later I began to take back the reins of my life. To date, I had not really given myself back to Him. I was trying to reclaim my faith, sweep out my house, and put it in order.

When the unclean spirit has gone out of a man, he passes through waterless places seeking rest, but he finds none. Then he says, 'I will return to my house from which I came.' And when he comes he finds it empty, swept, and put in order. Then he goes and brings with him seven other spirits more evil than himself, and they enter and dwell there; and the last state of that man becomes worse than the first. So shall it be also with this evil generation (Matt. 12:43–45).

Jeremiah describes the process that had been set into motion: "My people have committed two evils: they have forsaken me, the fountain of living waters, and hewed out cisterns for themselves, broken cisterns, that can hold no water" (2:13).

All my attempts at creating a meaningful ministry were like pouring water into a broken cistern.

I became a renewal "junkie." I rushed out to buy every book that claimed to have a plan or a theology for the renewal of the church. In my pursuit of the perfect plan for renewal in my doctoral studies, I surveyed two hundred local church clergy. That research showed the key to vitality in the church was the pastor. When the pastor was spiritually dead, the church was spiritually dead. A depressed pastor usually had a depressed church. Out of the two hundred clergy who responded to the study, there were at least twenty who called themselves depressed. They expressed feelings of being trapped, frustrated, and discouraged about the prospects for their churches. Only three or four of these mainline church pastors identified renewal as having anything to do with the renewal that comes through the new life that Christ offers. It sounded as though there were scores of us mainline church clergy who were broken and cracked cisterns.

Another entry into the unoccupied spiritual house was the small group movement, which patterned itself after the encounter movement. The church was a "caring-sharing" community, they said. That caring and sharing was related only peripherally to Christ. There was one weekend we called "house church," organized by a professor and his wife from a Chicago area seminary. We were led through all kinds of exercises designed to free us from "hangups" and "inhibitions." Judi attended, but mostly to watch me, she said. "You need your inhibitions, John," she told me sarcastically after I expounded on how we should get rid of them all.

One exercise had us crawling around on the floor like newborn puppies. We were to bump into each other, wrestle on the floor, and generally discover the joy of being puppies. Judi wouldn't join the fun. When we were safe at home, I accused her of being uptight and overly hung up on outward appearances. Her response confirmed my suspicions: "John, I just don't see what crawling around on the floor like a bunch of ignorant dogs is supposed to have to do with the church!"

The difficulty in recalling all of this is that the church had to suffer through that bewildering time with me. After our "house church" weekend, the group that attended wanted to take over a Sunday morning worship service to convey some of the new and exciting things we had discovered. The beginning of the service consisted of passing out lemons to the whole congregation, and asking them to "get to know their lemons." The lemons were then put into paper bags and each person was asked to find their original lemon. This was our call to worship.

Almost everyone was as hung up about the lemons as Judi was about playing puppy! To this day people remember the "lemon Sunday" with a smile . . . sometimes a frown.

The pain in remembering this is that I cannot push it all off as something created by a few nutty lay people. I was right there at the center of things. This was the new, renewed, avant garde church. There was one approving young man who thought our lemon service was "far out."

The whole renewal movement was a flop. Scores of people in parish ministry, myself included, fairly wore out the church with continual studies of who we were, why we were, and what we were. The renewal movement simply masked the fact that thousands of churches and their clergy were empty and vacuous. The vacuum at the center of the life of these churches drew into it all manner of bizarre and blasphemous chaff. At best it was a disaster, and at worst, demonic. One dared not question, however, some of the activities that were engaged in on behalf of the renewal movement. The unpardonable sin of that movement was to be "hung up."

I lost two of my sharpest college students in the congregation to the Campus Crusade people. When I suggested rather patronizingly they were opting for simple answers to complex problems, they quickly responded, "It sure beats no answers, and that's what we've been getting. What is going on here never did anything to help me change my life."

I didn't question much at all. As my own inner emptiness increased, my outward life made less sense. The church wasn't renewed, and it wasn't growing. I wasn't renewed, and I was growing sick. The "fire in my bones" would surface only to fade again. I would discover something of the reality of Christ only to lose Him again.

I began to withdraw. I pulled into myself and away from relationships, pastoral work, and outside interests. Judi had decided to go back to school to get a college degree, and there seemed to be a silent agreement between us that we put our relationship on the shelf for the time being. We drifted farther apart, and I had a feeling our marriage would break up one day. I didn't know why or when, but I knew it would not last.

I turned to some specialized training in pastoral counseling, partly because I became more and more introspective, shutting out the world; partly as a search for what was wrong down inside me.

Johnny began to have difficulties more frequently during his sixth grade year. He was a behavior problem, unable to face his daily challenges. Counseling was suggested for him, but Judi and I were so wrapped up in our own lives that we delayed getting help. We also did not have the energy to deal with the problem. One visit to a school psychologist who was "cool," as Johnny said, simply ended with the advice that we support Johnny and "to heck with the school."

I kept up with pastoral work now in only a perfunctory way. I visited church members in the hospital, wrote sermons, and hid. I escaped to "study" and read because I had almost no energy. No one questions a pastor much about what he does. Parishoners assume we are very busy, and they don't want to bother us. We are very involved, they believe, praying, preparing sermons, visiting people, and studying. I was just barely managing to do some of those things.

I had very little left for the pulpit and struggled to concentrate so I could put my thoughts down on paper. As time wore on, I had to fight my way out of bed on Sunday mornings. I was getting more and more depressed and battling each day to keep my outward appearance intact. Inside, I was afraid that I was headed for a nervous breakdown. I was plagued alternately by depression and anxiety. When I wasn't fighting one, I was paralyzed by the other.

I made excuses to go home earlier in the day. Telling myself I was going home to study and to prepare my sermons, I would sit with a book in my lap, drinking to numb the feelings that were unstitching my personality. The anesthetic dulled my senses for a time, but the depression and anxiety always came back in double measure.

I was taking medication for high blood pressure without knowing that one of its side effects is depression. The medication, reserpine, can cause suicidal feelings in an already depressed person. Between my spiritual condition and the reserpine, life was unbearable. On a few occasions, I sat in our family room with no one at home, reading a book, drinking and crying.

There's simply no hope, I thought. *I've tried everything, and there's simply no meaning left in my life. I once had a faith, but it is gone. I'm sick of all this phony renewal stuff. I just cannot fill the deep void in my life!*

I felt like a hypocrite and a failure—a failure as a husband and a father. I couldn't bear to look at Judi some Sunday mornings as I stood in that pulpit. Keeping up the front was exhausting. There was, it seemed, no possible way out of this misery. All of my frustrations and hopelessness came to focus one evening when a barrier broke inside and a flood of bitterness, anger, and grief poured out in a torrent of tears.

"I've been through this all before! Too many times before. I *hate* my life. Damn it, *I hate my life!*" I yelled at the empty room. No one answered but a black wall of gloom that closed in around me. I wanted peace of mind more desperately than anything else. To be able to sleep and not wake up. . . .

I went to the medicine cabinet and took out my bottle

of reserpine. I reasoned that if one pill could reduce my blood pressure, then perhaps a handful would stop it altogether. I swallowed a dozen and went back to my chair in the den. Johnny was out, and Jaie and Joyce were already in bed. Judi was at a meeting with her women's group at school. I was very tired and began to drift off to sleep. *Do I want to live? Die? I don't know. Should I go try to throw up?* Thoughts gathered around my mind and images from the past thirty-some years drifted in and out of my consciousness.

Now darkness was coming. The longing for sleep swept over me in waves as I surrendered to unconsciousness.

14

Home Is in Sight

"John! John! Wake up. Why don't you go to bed?"

Judi's voice surprised me. I had thought I would never hear it again. I told her what had happened, and immediately she tried to get me to go to the hospital.

"No. Not that, Judi. I'll be okay. I don't want people to think I'm nuts, even if I am!"

I went upstairs and threw up. My head was hurting, and I felt sick all over. Inside and out I ached with some kind of malady that I couldn't describe. It was a combination of depression, emptiness, guilt, fear, and disgust.

Then the tiniest sliver of light broke through a corner of my consciousness somewhere and said, *I'm glad I didn't die.*

Judi and I have talked many times since that night

about that episode. "Do you think you really wanted to die, John?" she would ask.

"Do you think I really wanted to die, Judi?" I would ask her.

I don't know. To this day I don't know. We talked about the possibility that I would simply leave this part of the story out.

But this low point is crucial to the whole story. I believe there may be one other person out there, who has looked into the black emptiness of spiritual void and who might come to know that it is possible to live again, to have faith again, after the bottom seems to have dropped out of the universe.

Judi was very concerned that I get some kind of help. I resisted. I had a difficult time letting people behind my facade, and I did not like to share my pain or vulnerability. Besides, a pastor can't have problems.

I did go to a colleague who was also a clinical psychologist. He thought I was simply having a "vocational crisis." Perhaps a change of jobs was all that I needed. (I've discovered over the years that a desire for frequent change can be a sign of personal trouble. A new job, a new church, a new spouse, or a new city can be an attempt to cure an inner struggle. I was thinking about a new church as cure for my turmoil.)

I was at the point of an interview with a large church and had to make a decision. I was also close to acceptance in a clinical training program of a local hospital well known for the quality of its training. There were always more applicants than there were training positions. This would be a one year, full-time situation that offered the possibility of a new form of ministry.

I was in a crisis with this decision; as a matter of fact I had not been doing well with any decisions lately. I decided to take the new church and not the training. I called and bowed out of the clinical training residency.

Two days later I knew I had made the wrong decision. A new church would be another three- or four-year repeat of the same thing I was going through now. I called back the people at the hospital and asked to reapply for the residency. In spite of the indecision I had shown, which pointed to possible personal trouble, I was permitted to undertake the clinical training.

Although I saw Clinical Pastoral Education (CPE) as a means of seeking another form of ministry, God had other plans for my training.

15

Johnny

Johnny.

"Little Man."

Johnny was our "little man." He lived through everything with us. From the earliest days when there was joy and laughter all the time to the days of late where there was almost no joy and laughter, "little man" was a central part of our lives.

In the beginning years of our marriage, I would have claimed some credit for the success of the Kodak Company. If there is one place in the whole of my being that I am completely vulnerable, it is with Johnny. My heart is held together only by the glue of God's grace when it comes to the pain and sorrow that we have lived through with "little man."

We were vaguely aware that Johnny was headed for difficulty from about the time he was in sixth grade. We can see that much more clearly now, but could not and would not see it at the time. His difficulties began before my CPE residency in Chicago, but intensified severely while I was training at the hospital.

Just one week before my training began, Johnny walked out of the house and did not come home that evening.

The ringing of the phone brought a glimmer of hope for the promise of an answer to the question that had plagued our sleepless night: "Where could he be?" That question would find itself deeply ingrained in everything that happened in the life of our family over the next four years. In our dreams, our subconscious, our arguments, and our prayers, the question would almost become our existence. "Johnny, where are you?"

I answered the insistent 3 A.M. phone call.

"Hello, Reverend Jewell?"

"Yes, speaking."

"This is the Sheriff's Department at North Platte, Nebraska. We're holding your son for possession of marijuana and for hitchhiking on the interstate highway. We are willing to drop the charges if you will come and pick him up."

We decided that Judi would fly out and pick up Johnny, who was now in ninth grade. Though we were angry, frightened, and perplexed, we were hopeful this might become a good experience. There had been disturbing signs that not all was well with Johnny, but I was so heavily invested in my own struggles and Judi in her school work that we had little time left for a problem son. We had become defensive about suggestions that

Johnny go to a counselor and ducked our heads and hoped for the best.

Judi flew to Omaha and then drove out to North Platte to retrieve what we hoped would be a young man who had learned his lesson. Looking through a tiny opening into a dirty cell at a ragged and penitent boy, Judi choked back the tears and asked, "Do you want to come home with me or stay here?"

He, of course, said he had learned his lesson well and would like to come home. Once out on the highway and free from the confines of the county jail, Judi asked once again as we had agreed that she would. "Johnny, if you do not really want to be at home, I'll let you out right now. There is no sense forcing you to come home if you don't want to be there. We love you and we want you to be with us, but we won't force you and we won't keep coming to bail you out."

"I really want to come home," he replied.

There was some joy at home that next evening. We were a complete family around the dinner table. Those times of being together were more and more infrequent, but for this night we were grateful. We ate together, prayed together, and laughed through a few tears. Johnny affirmed that he had learned very clearly that running away is not the way to solve problems. He said he knew now how much his home meant to him.

It was a tough lesson, but a good one. The few hundred dollars in air fare, the tears, and the pain were worth it. As I lay in bed that evening, there was a good feeling that everyone was safely in bed, and with a heavy load of guilt, my prayers included thanks and my promise to pay more attention to what was going on with my family and less to my own personal struggles. I saw this episode as the end of a trying period.

But it wasn't the end. It was the beginning of a time of such pain that I am grateful I could not see what was coming. Johnny spent the major part of the next year away from home. I could never have handled a pastorate during that year and can see so very clearly now that God's reasons and my reasons for being in a year of clinical training were so very far apart. I was thinking of a new career; God knew very well that I could not have handled any career that year.

There were phone calls in the middle of the night. Sometimes they would be from Johnny saying he was okay, and sometimes they were from juvenile authorities asking what we wanted done with him. There were repeated flights home, in spite of our resolutions that we would not go through this again. There were a couple of reunions when the whole family felt that Johnny was home to stay, and then the heartbreak when Johnny ran again.

Strangely enough, Johnny always told us he loved us when he called. One evening he called, and after talking to us, talked to his younger brother, Jaie. Jaie broke up, and crying into the receiver, which was wet with his tears, he pleaded, "Johnny, please come home. I need you." Johnny cried on the other end. We cried in our pillows after everyone else was in bed.

We were never sure whether there would be a complete

family when holidays came. At Thanksgiving there was an empty chair where Johnny was supposed to sit, and nothing tasted very good to me and my heart had very little thanks in it. Christmas he was home, but by the middle of January he was gone again.

We prayed, we went to counseling with the whole family, we sought advice, and we analyzed. My prayers consisted of a lot of crying out *"Why?"*

Judi and I grew even farther apart. I was building a sense of anger toward her, imagining that Johnny's difficulties were somehow her fault. Or were they my fault? Perhaps they weren't anybody's fault. It was very confusing. Why was all this happening? No matter whose fault it was, however, I was now sure when things settled down somewhat I would divorce her.

We discovered during this whole process that a significant number of marriages are wrecked on the shoals of problem children. Whether the problems are physical or emotional, difficulty with children places incredible pressures on a family and a marriage. Dear friends of ours lost two boys to cystic fibrosis and told us that over ninety percent of parents of children with this disease wind up divorced.

While blaming Judi for Johnny's trouble, I was fighting off the recognition that Johnny was in some way living out in his outward life the chaos and turmoil that I had been living internally for years. My spiritual storms were played out in his life. During the time of my clinical training, I worked with adolescents in a psychiatric unit and could see that same dynamic in the lives of those young people. Children will very often act out the stress in the marriage relationship of their parents.

There was a long period of time when we heard nothing at all from Johnny. We were not sure whether he was dead or alive. When the phone rang our hearts jumped, and when the door bell sounded we raced to the door with the hope that it just might be him. Not knowing was the most difficult thing of all.

One day a startling thought entered my mind and sent chills down my spine. *It would be better if the phone would ring and someone would tell us that Johnny had been found dead,* I thought. The experience we were going through was worse than grief, because there was never any resolution. I would find myself getting interested or involved in something only to have Johnny come crashing into my consciousness. "Where are you, Johnny?" Alternately, I would grieve and then try to get on with living, but Judi would be grieving when I was trying to forget. At least if we could bury him, we could get the grieving over with and then get on with whatever life was going to bring. As it was, it seemed he died a hundred times.

As we lived with the pain at home, I saw pain and misery in the lives of hundreds of people at the hospital. The psychiatric unit, the alcohol and drug treatment unit, and the coronary and intensive care units opened my eyes to a dimension of human suffering I had never experienced. There were times when that pain and misery made my own difficulties seem so small in comparison.

There were other times, however, when they only intensified mine. In any case, I was bound with others through
suffering in a way I could not have even imagined.

When I shared an evening with brokenhearted parents, there was a bond between us that was almost awe-
some. I cannot count the number of times I sat with and
prayed with parents who had lost young children or teen-
agers. How they would reach out for some tiny glimmer
of assurance that there was a God who cared about what
was happening to them, who would care for those lost
children!

One couple lost a seventeen-year-old boy in a drown-
ing accident. When I was called to the emergency room I
was told the couple was on the way in; they did not know
the boy had died. In the fifteen minutes before they arrived I felt as though I were deeply connected with them.
I was almost with them, driving to the hospital in a panic, only I felt I had received the call and it was Johnny in
place of their boy. It was I racing along the streets not
knowing what had really happened or why.

They finally arrived and were brought to a small conference room where I had been waiting, praying fervent-
ly. I was praying a lot these days, forced to my knees with
the suffering I was seeing and sharing.

The parents must have seen in my face the tremendous
shock and grief of what it means to lose a son. They both
began to cry.

"I'm sorry," I said.

The grief came in waves, like the pounding of wild
surf. Their questions followed in a torrent mixed with

tears, moaning, and anguish. "What happened? Why? Who was responsible?"

They were quiet for a time, their tears flowing like a gentle stream. Then in anguish they cried out, "How could God let this happen?"

The question was too much for my own composure. Tears began to form in my eyes and then spilled down my face. "I wish I knew; I really wish I knew," I said. "I don't know why things happen the way they do at all. I only trust that whatever else is going on, God knows about the pain. He lost His own Son."

Finally the couple asked to see the boy, and we went together into a room where the boy's lifeless body had been placed on a pallet.

Another giant wave of grief came. The three of us were locked in a huddle, hanging on as though there was a great earthquake trying to knock us down. For several moments there were no words; only tears. I was bound with them. I could almost see Johnny's lifeless body lying in some hospital room. He never carried any identification, I remembered. No one would know whom to call if they found him dead.

I prayed with the parents and remained with them for a time. They asked how it was that I was crying, too, when I did not even know them. I told them something about Johnny, something very brief about our own pain, and how I didn't know whether my son was alive or not.

A few weeks later, I received a note from them telling of their deep appreciation for the time we spent together, and how they would always remember that experience. It had been a sacred time for me, too. Much had been going on within me during that year of clinical training to open up my heart and mind. As the difficulty with Johnny and the misery I was seeing in the lives of others weighed heavier and heavier, I began more and more to seek the strength of God for my own life. I felt a sense of brokenness and inadequacy I had never encountered before. In the face of suffering I could do absolutely nothing about, I could only beg the mercy of God for the people whose lives were touching mine. My own life was filled with things I could do nothing about.

There was an increasing awareness in my life that God's own Son was bound intimately with us through suffering and trial. Though my own life was in tremendous turmoil and the lives of the patients I worked with were lived on stormy seas, a certain calm began to grow within. As I felt more and more helpless and broken, more and more I found myself going to God with my pain. I didn't have a plan for God to accomplish for me now, and I gave up telling Him what should be done with Johnny. I also quit asking Him to change Judi. Most of what I was doing in my prayer life was crying and saying things like "Please" and "Help!"

God had me where He wanted me.

A phone call from California initiated the most devastating experience of my life. Johnny had been picked up by juvenile authorities. We had not heard a word from him for four months. I had almost accepted the fact that he might be dead; it wasn't like him not to call every once in a while.

I was at the hospital getting ready to say good-bye to

the clinical training group. Our time was almost over and the year completed. I had planned on getting on with the next phase of life. The call came in the middle of everything, and my mind went reeling. I did not hear the first few sentences the officer spoke, but then the words broke through: "Your son has needle marks in his veins. He's incoherent . . . most likely psychotic. Do you want him?"

Did I want him? I worked with lots of kids whose parents didn't want them. Juvenile workers who pick up kids like Johnny will almost automatically assume that they are not wanted.

I didn't! If there had been some way to say there was a mistake, that this wasn't my boy, I would have done that. Of course I didn't want him, not this way.

"I will have to talk it over with my wife," I answered the officer. "I will call you back tomorrow morning."

Over the past three or four months, along with some internal quiet that had come my way, had also come an appreciation for Judi. The work with the people at the hospital, along with the working out of some of the painful issues of my own life, had given me a new sense of care for her. It was not the innocent love that I had had for her in the beginning, but a more mature love. I wondered if it was the kind of love that Adam might have had for Eve after their eviction from Eden: the love that comes with the bonding of two lives in the "pain of child-bearing" and "sweat of the brow" realities of life and sin in this grieving world.

Judi and I agreed we would send just one more airline

ticket and bring him home. There was, however, no joy in our news about Johnny. We decided we would make the commitment to do everything in our power to help him this one last time. We were already so much in debt with the expenses of the past year or so, one more bill wouldn't make that much difference. Perhaps we had not gone the limit. We would both feel much better about ourselves if we tried to help him "just once more."

The next afternoon Judi and I drove to O'Hare airport to pick him up. When Johnny left us he weighed 155 pounds and was a strong, strapping kid. The shadow of a kid who emerged from the jetway caused Judi to collapse against the wall, while I stood in shock, unable to move. The long-haired, 105-pound, emaciated boy who came toward us had two blank places where there used to be bright, sparkling eyes. He was a physical and psychological wreck. Judi ran to him and took him in her arms, crying uncontrollably. From a distance I could see his head draped over Judi's shoulder, and there was no response in his eyes. No pain, no guilt, no fear, no joy—there was *nothing* there.

I made an excuse to Judi that I wanted to go to the men's room. I ran to a stall and vomited and cried and pounded on the walls. The sight of my son made me so sick to my stomach that inside something cracked and shattered. I don't know what it was, but it was smashed into a thousand pieces. My closest guess is that it was my heart of stone, which had begun to wear down some time before.

I took Judi home first, then drove Johnny to the hospital, where I had arranged for him to be admitted to the psychiatric unit. Johnny was silent, obviously off in the strange world that occupied his mind.

"Are you hungry?" I asked him.

"Huh? I don't know, I went through a blue triangle . . . there was fire all over . . . cartoons were alive and I was shot. . . ." He babbled on.

I took him into the hospital and bought him a candy bar, which he consumed in two bites. He ate the box after he finished the candy. When he had been taken to his room, I went out to the car to head home.

Before I reached the first intersection, I could not see the road. The tears poured out of the emptiness that had been my lot for the past few years. I collapsed over the steering wheel, eased the car to the side of the road, and turned off the motor. I shook and sobbed with the most intensive anguish of guilt and grief I had ever known. I did not know a human being could hurt so profoundly without dying.

I kept picturing this child, who at two years of age would try to sing the hymn of invitation where I had preached my first sermons. He was bright, lively, and always very, very happy. He loved everyone, knew no strangers, and everyone loved him. As a baby, he went to strangers with outstretched arms and a smile.

I shuddered and my body ached. Animal groans emerged from my throat. Beaten! I was totally and thoroughly beaten. Nothing and no one had ever had me in a position like this in my entire life.

It was half an hour before I regained enough composure to think about driving the rest of the way home.

Suddenly there was a stillness inside me, a quiet that I did not want to disturb. I sat motionless and waited. The pain had subsided, and I was calm inside. I could almost hear a voice:

> *O dear God, once I could see,*
> *but now I am blind!*

I had no idea what would happen to Johnny or to my ministry. But I knew I had a desperate need, and that there was no way out except to throw myself totally and completely on the mercy of God.

The doctor had explained to me that the massive doses of amphetamines Johnny had mainlined might have destroyed some of his neurological system.

"When will he come out of this?" I asked.

"He might never come out of it." The doctor's response struck like cold steel to the core of my heart.

I managed to make it home that night, but I was in a fog. I knew the direction of my life was changed forever. I did not know how long it would take or what this would all mean, but there were no choices left. I wanted desperately to be back at home in the arms of the One who had touched me seventeen years earlier.

There had been so many times during the past ten years when I wanted to be back home, but tenaciously insisted on keeping control of the process. I had tried to build my own spiritual house, forgetting that "Unless the LORD builds the house, those who build it labor in vain . . ." (Ps. 127:1).

I knew now, at this very moment, I could not build a

thing and that there was no possible way I could do anything to gain back the faith I once had. It would have to be a gift from God. It would have to come when I opened my eyes to the fact that what had taken place over the years was not accidental. I had willfully and stubbornly persisted in walking into a spiritual far country. My departure from an authentic biblical faith was *sin*.

The most painful thing I've ever done in my life is to park my car in the lot of the townhouse Judi and I had rented for my training year and sit there with my son a psychiatric vegetable, thinking: "This is all largely the product of the sin in my life!"

At first, I wanted to talk myself out of that thought. "Sin?" The fact is, the realization still hurts. It will hurt until the day I die. God had to use a window of tremendous vulnerability to get hold of my life once again.

My journey and my desertion of the faith was a *willful* decision. I *chose* the bondage of the world.

Some very dear friends would try to comfort me.

"Oh, c'mon, John, all of us have to grow and mature. You're no different. You couldn't have avoided all this."

But down inside, down there where I am honest and free from the desire to hide what has happened with my life, I know this one thing: When I ask myself whether my journey might have been avoided, I have to answer yes.

The only remedy for sin is repentance. Even that hurts. One finds peace with God once again only when he completely turns around.

Jeremiah spoke for me that night:

Behold the storm of the LORD!
  Wrath has gone forth a whirling tempest;
it will burst upon
  the head of the wicked.
The fierce anger of the LORD
    will not turn back
    until he has executed and accomplished
    the intents of his mind.
In the latter days
  you will understand this
(Jer. 30:23,24).

There had been no room at all for this judging dimension of God's sovereignty during the past few years in my theology. But, thankfully, God broke through the intellectual pride and rebellion by smashing my life until I could reach out once again for His healing.

"For after I had turned away I repented;
and after I was instructed, I
    smote upon my thigh.
I was ashamed, and I was confounded,
    because I bore the disgrace of
      my youth"
(Jer. 31:19).

Sitting in the car that night, face to face with the truth, I prayed, "Lord, I surrender. I am a foolish, stubborn, and willful child. I am broken and beaten. I do not know if You have any use for me at all or what You want to do with me, but I am Yours. I am Humpty Dumpty, and there is nothing in all of the past ten years that can put me back together again.''

My tears poured out again, in a river that was refreshing, cleansing, and healing. These were not the tears of bitterness that I had lived with for the past years. I was suffering anguish and hurt, but now I knew healing, too. Even my profound pain was built upon a joy that supports and surrounds anyone who will surrender to the everlasting, healing love of the Father.

I continued praying as I walked to the door, ''. . . and O dear God, if I cannot know that You are close beside me every single moment of my life from this day on, then I don't think I want to walk another step. If I can't love You and serve You each and every day from this moment, then I think I would just as soon die right here and now.''

I knew I was home! I wasn't exempt from the pain yet to come or from the pain of wondering what might have been in my ministry over the past ten years . . . but I was home.

"But when he came to himself he said, '. . . I will arise and go to my father, and I will say to him, "Father, I have sinned against heaven and before you; I am no longer worthy to be called your son. . . ."' And he arose and came to his father . . ." *(Luke 15:17–20).*

16

Falling in Love Again

"Whose little boy are you?"

I could recall that question from the earliest days of my memories. I stood just higher than my father's knee in a forest of men who seemed just shorter than the clouds which drifted overhead. Dad and his mining engineer friends were deep in discussion; probably about a great body of ore about to be discovered under the earth. One of the men stooped to talk with me and asked, "Whose little boy are you?"

"His," I answered, pointing upward to the man whose leg my other arm was firmly wrapped around. "I belong to him."

Having found—or perhaps better, having *been found* by my heavenly Father—I wanted to hang on tight and never stray again. The return of a sense of being more fully alive came almost instantly with my surrender to God—a sense of joy that I had forgotten. It was as though I had been fighting and choking out in the ocean, trying to get to shore, and then had been handed a life preserver. I had emerged from a long period of being lost in a fog.

Clarity about that fog and about the intense unhappiness that had possessed my life for so long came with a complete turning back toward the Father. It came with repentance. Eugene O'Neill captures the sense of what it is like to lose one's faith in his tragic play, *Long Day's Journey Into Night*. In the play, the mother, Mary, has had an emotional breakdown, which resurfaces at the end of the play. She is wandering aimlessly about the house with a sense that she has lost something and says:

> What is it I'm looking for? I know it's something I lost. [She continues in spite of the family's hopeless attempts to bring her back.] Something I need terribly. I remember when I had it I was never lonely or afraid. I can't have lost it forever, I would die if I thought that. Because then there would be no hope.[1]

The whole play is a profoundly moving expression of lost humanity. The sheer dread of the condition that I had lived for the past few years keeps me hanging on tight to God.

"Whose little boy are you?" There's no hesitancy about that now. "I belong to Jesus Christ!"

I had searched for years, for I knew I had lost something very precious, but I had never been able to remember exactly what it was I had lost. The joy of faith is a fruit of the Spirit (see Gal. 5:22). Once you have begun to live apart from the Spirit, the Holy Spirit is grieved and that joy is no longer possible. The real joy of faith will only be a faint recollection.

It is not possible to think your way back to that joy, for it is only God's to give back. The psalmist prayed, "Restore to me the joy of thy salvation . . ." (Ps. 51:12). The condition of the one who has lost faith is worse than that of the person who has never known Jesus Christ. The emptiness is doubled. There is the emptiness of life apart from Christ and the emptiness that can only faintly remember fullness. That emptiness had created for me the most incredible vacuum which drew into it a sickness almost unto death.

Though there was an abundance of pain yet to come, I was able to say in spite of that pain the exact opposite of what I had cried out one night not too long before: "I *love* my life!" Thanks to the never failing love of God, which waits at the gate for returning children, I fell in love again . . . with life!

I had brand new eyes for Judi, too. I was amazed at the way she had lived through all of the pain and turmoil. As we sat together one evening in our family room, I stopped to look at her. She was reading. My heart spilled over with love for her. *Thank You, God . . . thank You for Judi,* I thought.

Tell her, dummy! came another thought. Not easy for me to do, but here goes. . . .

"I love you, Judi. Do you know that? Do you know that I've fallen in love with you again? God gave you to me, you know."

She just smiled.

She knows? I wondered. *She knows. Wow! How incredible.* I kept sneaking glances at her that night. *The lady with the black leotards and the bongo drums!*

During the last few months of my clinical training, the "fire in my bones" began to burn more and more. With each new experience of seeing people in the grip of intense physical and emotional suffering, I wanted to be back on the firing line. The place to be was where there was opportunity to reach people before the breakdowns came.

I had begun to struggle with the future half way through my program. The options were to pursue additional training to become a CPE supervisor, to take another year of training in pastoral psychotherapy and to work as a full-time counselor, or to return to parish ministry. My supervisor was helpful in clarifying the direction I would take.

"What's the greatest experience of your life, John?" he asked.

"Honestly?"

"Yeah. What is it that has given you more joy than anything else?"

"Preaching!"

"Then why in the world would you want to do anything else?" he asked.

That was it. I began to look for a pulpit before the end of the year and was called to serve a church in a beautiful area in Chicago. My predecessor had been the church's only pastor of memory, with a forty-seven-year pastorate. He was also a classic liberal. From notes in books, tapes of sermons, and conversations with parishoners, it was evident he was not clear at all about the person and saving ministry of Jesus Christ. The people were the most spiritually hungry I had ever encountered! Their spirits were parched and longing for the water of life, ". . . as in a dry and weary land where no water is" (Ps. 63:1).

Shortly after I had begun my ministry with this church, I preached a sermon on the woman who had been ill for years and then reached out to touch the hem of Jesus' garment. A sense came over me that had come upon me that night so many years ago when the love of Christ poured over the congregation. I felt an urgency to issue an invitation for them to respond to the gospel. Jesus' compassion on the sheep who were without a shepherd possessed my own spirit.

And yet, I was terrified. These people had sat under a liberal preacher for forty-seven years. They were almost paranoid about anything even remotely resembling the "born again" people. The mention of Billy Graham was enough to send them into hiding. So what to do?

I was compelled to call for a response to the gospel. The difference was so clear to me now between a lecture from the pulpit and preaching from the pulpit. I had lectured for years, but here the Word of God broke through the words of a sermon, and it seemed very natural to call for a response.

My voice trembling, I began my pastoral prayer at the end of the sermon. "Somehow, Jesus, You are passing through this place today as You passed through that town in Palestine so long ago. There are so many of us who desperately need to reach out and touch You as that woman did. We too, are afraid. Yet, our hearts are broken and our spirits so hungry for Your touch. Jesus, as a symbol of our wanting Your power in our lives, some of us are going to lift our hands right now as though we were reaching out to You. Some of us have never really touched You, and we want to say that our lives are empty without You. For the very first time we would reach out to You and give ourselves to You in faith. Please see us and touch us now, Lord, as people around the sanctuary today lift their hand to You."

The church was silent—utterly still. My heart was beating so fast I was sure the choir could hear it.

After what seemed to me like a half hour, but which was in reality about twenty seconds, a hand went up. "God bless you," I said.

Now another hand. And another. Tears began to flow from people's eyes. Handkerchiefs emerged from pockets all over the sanctuary.

One young man with whom I had recently spent several hours was critically ill. He was having a real struggle with faith and could not say he believed. He lifted his head, looked me straight in the eye, and raised his hand.

There were tears in his eyes. His response brought tears to my eyes, too.

There was Johnny, out of the hospital now for a few months and doing well. His hand went up and tears came to his eyes. *Little man, too,* I thought. And the handkerchief came out of my pocket.

One woman had been asked by an usher at the beginning of the service to move her car from in front of a neighbor's drive. She told me later she started to go back to her home, but something compelled her to return to church. She was too embarrassed to come back to the sanctuary to be seated, so she listened from the vestibule. I found her in tears after the service. "I've never touched Him in my life like that!" she said.

That Sunday was a turning point in the life of our church. Jesus Christ moved into the dry and thirsty land of that congregation like a mighty river of the water of life. On my way home after that service, I was walking ten feet above the sidewalk. "I love You! I love You!" my heart was screaming to the Lord. I wanted to shout it out loud.

They say that people who experience the new birth sometimes get carried away. Judi felt like that about me for a time after I had first met Christ. But there is an experience that just may be even more powerful. That is the experience of being born again *again,* as it were! I was in love with preaching and in love with Jesus Christ in a whole new way.

When our church began to feel the power of the Spirit in our midst, I wanted to begin making the Bible an integral part of what our church was all about. One of the members told me that Bible classes had never gone over in that church, but I tried one anyway. The class grew from eight or ten to forty people over the year. A great hunger for the Scriptures began to grow and in my own life there was a return of the spark in my own reading. I was in love with the Bible again!

I was also in love again with the purpose of the gospel. My heart was broken again for all those people who struggle and find themselves in such misery and heart-break all over this land but do not know that there is a Savior who can bring healing. Perhaps my journey brought an even greater sense of that need. Having tried so many ways, I was in love again with the beautiful simplicity of this one statement: ". . . There is no other name under heaven given among men by which we must be saved" (Acts 4:12).

17

Just To Be Sure

Johnny spent the whole summer in the hospital after he returned from California. It was a hard time for all of us. I had just begun my new parish ministry after clinical training, Judi was teaching, and Johnny's stay in the hospital required our constant attention. His psychiatrist—a marvelous person, a terrific doctor, and a committed Christian—wanted us to be with Johnny every possible moment. He gave orders to the staff that we were to be called at any time, even in the middle of the night, if there were problems with him.

"I want him fully and completely to know you two and what you stand for, and to decide whether he's going to make his home with you or not," he told us. "I almost wish I could admit both of you so that Johnny would have to deal with you. He's been running for years, and he will have to decide whether he wants a home with you."

Throughout June, July, August, and September we visited, counseled, grieved, and cried. Johnny's progress was slow, but he was getting better. His mind was clearing, and he was gaining weight. He began to talk about wanting to be at home with the family. He asked for "Marky" and "Jimmy." We had almost forgotten. Marky and Jimmy were two monkeys a friend had made out of winter socks. They had been his favorite possessions when he was about five or six years old.

"I want to ask you for something," he said, "but I'm afraid you'll think I'm stupid."

"No, we won't, Johnny. What is it?"

"I wish I had Marky and Jimmy here with me!"

We all laughed! Johnny was regaining his emotions. "That felt great," he said. "Now if I could just get really mad!"

We went through a crisis when Johnny vowed that he would not continue in treatment and signed himself out of the hospital. There was a twenty-four-hour waiting period before he could leave legally. This was to give time for the physician to file formal commitment papers if he felt that was necessary. If Johnny would not rescind his decision, we would be forced to consign him to the back ward of a state hospital. He intended to force us into letting him come home or else he simply would leave and be on his own.

Johnny's psychiatrist was insistent that we not give in to his demands. "You can't let him go home in the shape he's in," he said. "That would be a disaster for the whole family. If he persists and won't accept treatment, then at least he won't kill himself in the state hospital."

We went to Johnny's room just once more and pleaded with him to stay for the remainder of his treatment.

"No! No! I'm okay now. I know I am. Please let me come home. I hate this place. It's this place that's driving me nuts!" He was crying so hard he was shaking from head to foot.

"No," Judi said. "We love you, Johnny, but we can't let you come home unless you finish your treatment. If you don't rescind your intention to sign out, we will commit you to the state hospital and you won't get any help there. You could spend the rest of your life there."

"No, I won't do it," he yelled. "I'll get out of here and run away!"

As we walked out of the room, the door locked behind us. We glanced back through the glass at Johnny's form shaking and crying on a bed with no sheet. There was only the bed in the middle of the locked, barren room. We might not see him again except for a hearing to commit him to the state hospital.

"All for nothing," Judi was sobbing, "all for nothing. John, we've gone through all of this for nothing." Her pain tore me apart. I hung onto her as she moaned, "Oh, my God, how can I leave my little boy locked up in a state hospital? It hurts so much to turn my back on him!"

We went to visit with some close friends. Jim and Joann had suffered a lot of grief with their own family, and he was also a pastor. We felt comfortable when we were with them because of their real, down-to-earth faith. We had called to say we were exhausted and needed to visit and have some diversion.

While we were talking around a picnic table in their backyard, Jim said, "Let's pray for Johnny right now. Let's ask God to reach out and touch him." I felt so much emotional pain I didn't know if I could take any more, but we prayed and we felt a great sense of relief.

As we drove home I said, "Judi, I don't think it's all for nothing—even if he has to go to the state hospital. We could never have lived with ourselves if we had not done everything we could. Besides, I'm discovering just how much I really love you in all of this!"

We slept more peacefully than we had for some time that night, but not for long. The phone rang at 2:00 A.M. When I answered, a nurse from the hospital was on the line.

"John wants to rescind his request for release. Do you want to come over?"

We went . . . with Marky and Jim!

A softer and quieter dimension entered my life during this time. With parish ministry, new things happening with people's faith, and a family in turmoil, I had to lean more on Christ and less on myself. I was so much more sure of Jesus, but not sure at all of myself. I felt weak and inadequate, and I discovered that it was precisely in this weakness that my strength from God would have to come. I had always loved the "yea though I walk through the valley" and the "my grace is sufficient for you" themes of Scripture. I had used them so often with others who were struggling and crushed by life and guilt. I knew those themes well, in my head.

In my heart, I had always been self-sufficient, holding tightly to that tiny cord which was the reins of my being. I kept that one seemingly insignificant vestige of control in reserve: the Achilles' heel of my spiritual life.

Now God had me once again. I do not presume to know the mind of God, but my deep conviction now is that God knew exactly what He was doing by giving me this whole situation. I don't believe He caused Johnny to become an addict and a runaway so that I would come home to Him. But somehow, as long as there are Johnny's in this world, I might be a person who needed one. St. Paul's words were now living realities for my spiritual survival: "For the sake of Christ, then, I am content with weaknesses, insults, hardships, persecutions, and calamities; for when I am weak, then I am strong" (2 Cor. 12:10).

I knew all of this intellectually, but now my life depended on it. Paul spoke in his letter to the Corinthians about a "man who was in Christ" who had been caught up to "the third heaven" some fourteen years earlier. He had heard "unspeakable words" (KJV) and could boast about a man like that. Instead, he boasted only of his weaknesses (see 2 Cor. 12:1–10).

I was a man like that—one who came to know Christ and things inexpressible. Now I could finally trust through my weaknesses, for they were the channels through which Christ could manifest His power! This passage became my "recovery passage."

I find that I am in need of daily prayer for my Achilles' heel to stay exposed and vulnerable, lest I stray. I am in no way one hundred percent faithful about that prayer for grace, but I can tell very quickly when I drift too far from grace. My life begins to get anxious, and my stomach begins to churn with all that "I" have to get done.

How beautiful the grace of God! It is as rain to one who, stranded in the desert, is near death for lack of water.

One more experience with Johnny would cement my own spiritual recovery. The severe wounds had begun to heal. Although I suffered an array of emotional and spiritual scars, I had begun to see how all of this could "work for good." People who were having family difficulties and who had been deeply hurt in the process of raising their children were coming to me with openness, sensing, I am sure, the empathy borne of my own wounding. Johnny was doing well, and I was confident that he would finally be okay. I felt as though the pieces were at last going to fit together.

One more crushing, devastating experience would bump my wound, knock off the scab, and I would bleed once again. I would be shocked at the depths of my grief and be driven still further into the arms of Christ. This would sever the last tiny strand of control of my life. Again, I can't second-guess what God was doing, but something deep inside me tells me He just wanted to make sure I was His.

Johnny was accepted in a special school where he could receive the help he needed to get his high school education back on track again. Judi and I were very grateful.

During the first few months at home after his hospitalization, we were extremely strict with him. Not only did he want Marky and Jimmy, his monkeys, in the hospital with him, but also he seemed to re-experience the whole of his childhood and early adolescence. We discovered that if we pretended he was six years old, then seven and eight and on up, we had a firm grip on what was happening with him. We watched with amazement as he proceeded in a few short months through a maturation process, as though he had to iron out all the kinks.

We were delighted with his progress. There were conflicts and times when we had to come down very hard on slips, when he would smoke marijuana and when he would break curfew, but the long haul was on an upward turn.

Eventually a semblance of normalcy returned to our home. We almost relaxed. If you have ever been through extreme pain with troubled children, then you will know just how long the healing process takes. Even after months or perhaps even years of seeming progress, in one tiny corner lurks the horrifying possibility that this could all come apart like the unraveling of a knit sweater.

We were, however, beginning to trust Johnny. He was becoming more responsible for his actions, and we had the fantastic news that as far as his doctor could tell, there were no residual effects from the drug experience.

He was enthusiastic and active in his life of faith. He told us that in the darkest hours of his addiction, he always saw Jesus Christ as the hope of any healing. "Somehow, I could not reach out, but I know now that without Jesus, I would have died out there somewhere!" he said to me one night.

The time came when Johnny wanted a job so he could earn some spending money. We had seen him grow to what seemed to us to be an almost normal teen, so we allowed him to look for a job. He came home to say he had found a job in a fast food restaurant. "Can I work tonight?" he asked. "The manager wants me to start tonight. If I can, the job's mine."

"Okay, Johnny," I said, "you can start. What time will you be home?"

"I'll be home about midnight. The buses come at fifteen to twelve." He kissed us and went off to work with a cheerful, "See you later!"

I began to watch the buses at midnight. We could see every bus as it came past our house from the window of the den. I was still looking at those buses when 2:00 A.M. came. Judi had gone to bed, and I said I would wait for Johnny. I knew the kids sometimes had to stay late in this twenty-four-hour place.

I tried to read, but I jumped from my chair every time I heard a bus rumble by the house. It was always empty, and it always went past the bus stop right across the street. The bright lights inside the bus told the story of whether Johnny was inside.

Three A.M. The buses stopped coming. I was possessed

by a cold and terrifying fear. I decided to drive to the restaurant and bring Johnny home. The past several months flashed through my mind as I made my way down the deserted streets. I pulled into the parking lot of the restaurant and sat in the car for five or ten minutes. I prayed that he would be in that place, but I was terrified I would find a disaster.

When I opened the door, my eyes were going a hundred miles an hour darting here and there to see where Johnny was. I couldn't find him and searched out the manager.

"Do you have a John Jewell working here?"

My mind was screaming as I barely heard the manager's single word that threatened to shatter my soul once again.

"Who?"

He had never heard of Johnny. I drove home barely able to see through the tears and with no time to spare in rushing to the bathroom.

I could not believe the pain. I had never hurt this bad. In my dreams after that night I saw Johnny off in the distance and I screamed and called to him, but he never saw me. He had only three days to get back to school before he would lose all credit for the semester.

In one dream I saw him with the orange robe of a cult and his hair was shaved. I was crying to him and yelling, "Johnny, please come back. Please come back before it's too late; before you lose all your credit!"

We were not to hear from him for two months. I woke up one night with such chest pains that I thought I would have to call an ambulance. I could not breathe without difficulty, and the pain was radiating down my left arm. "If this doesn't stop soon, I'll have to wake Judi. My God, am I dying?"

I walked to the den, rubbing my chest, and looked out the window. A clock I had built chimed out 2:00 A.M. I had stood here a few days earlier looking for him at 2:00 A.M.

A dam broke down inside. Tears flooded out like a river, and the pain in my chest stopped. I had been trying to hold in a severe grief that I was afraid could literally kill me. I had tried during all of this to make my heart hard. I didn't want to think about how much I loved this kid that I could not help and could not reach. I felt the waves of guilt pounding once again. What had I done?

"O God, is there no bottom to this well of grief? Why? Why do I have to love him so? Oh, please, if You would only take my feeling for him away!" I choked and growled and groaned without words in a frenzied, frightened praying from down inside of me where there were no words.

Then something happened.

I know that a tape recorder would not have picked up the words, but I heard them as clearly as if they had been audible.

"John, if I could give you a reason, an answer to your 'why,' would that help? It isn't an answer to your questions, but a balm for your heart that I can give you to calm the pain. I know it hurts. I know what it is like to lose a son. I've known heartbreak and I've longed for your return home to Me as you long for your son's return home. Let Me love you, not with answers for your mind, but with healing.''

With the voice came a profound presence in that den. The room was filled with something I had never experienced in my life before. It was as though God took the very first experience of Him I had ever known—the time when I came to know Jesus Christ as my Lord— and drove it deeper and more securely into the last cracks and crevices of my soul.

And with the voice and the presence came a picture in my mind. A vision? I would not go so far as to claim so, but what I saw was as real as the pictures that hang on the wall of my den. I could see a man standing by a gate in a rustic setting. It was the face that stood out.

There were lines in the face that seemed to be etched there by pain and heartbreak, and yet there was a tenderness that seemed to say there was nothing in all of the world this Man could not understand. His eyes reached out and touched the depths of my soul, as His arms reached out to touch me and gently enfold me in a care that is too profound for words. I reached back with my own arms shaking and my heart aching for the love that I could feel as the tears came from His eyes.

In the most real sense, I collapsed into the arms of this Waiting Presence; a Presence that I suddenly knew had been there all along, waiting.

"Welcome home, son. Welcome home."

"But why, Lord? Why all this hurt?"

"Just to be sure, son. Just to be sure."

18

Rebuilding Foundations

I will never be able to communicate fully the sheer joy of having been able to touch once again the splendor of knowing Christ in this life after having lost that faith at one time. Words fail every time I try to share the experience. Each day is a bonus day. Every experience of seeing another human being come alive in Jesus Christ is an unspeakable delight and a profoundly humbling event. That I should still have more children in Christ is a matter of utter amazement to my heart.

Life without Christ is unbearable after knowing life with Christ. I do spend time wondering what might have been, grieving for the harvest that was left in the field and wishing that it all might have been different. Even in the writing of my journey experience, there were so many times of saying, "If I could only go back to that time." St. Paul comes to my aid with profound spiritual and psychological insight, ". . . forgetting what lies behind and straining forward to what lies ahead, I press on toward the goal for the prize of the upward call of God in Christ Jesus" (Phil. 3:13,14).

Twenty years ago, I listened attentively to the senior pastor of our church preach a sermon called, "Why every preacher should go to hell!" Standing on this side of the journey to the far country and back again, I can feel that message again so strongly. I tremble when I think of life without Christ and how the pain was so incredibly intensified by the memory of life with Him. I tremble even more so when I think of and pray for friends who journeyed with me for a time and who are still out in the far country somewhere.

Every now and then I hear one of my brethren rather glibly say, "People like that just need to get down on their knees and get right with God," as though it were a very simple thing to regain what was lost. When I talk with people who are stuck out there in the far country, I usually come home, hit my knees, and weep for them. And I tremble once again as I wonder, "Could this be a taste of that horror which is the 'second death'?"

I simply cannot judge those who are still lost out there with that "younger son." I can only affirm the Father waits with open arms that ache with longing for the return of the children who have left His home. I want to stand up somewhere and cry out, "Come home! Come home! He loves us still. There is grace and mercy and—

most of all—peace. Peace like you never thought you would have again.''

My broken heart for those who know what it is to lose a faith that once gave meaning to life, is now God's gift to me. It is also the cornerstone of the new foundation under construction in my life. A solid, firm foundation that stands on His grace and promises, rather than on the shaky timbers of my poor design.

Early in my return to parish ministry and to the pulpit, I attended a conference for pastors intended for inspiration and renewal. While there with my friend Jim, who had prayed with us in his backyard during Johnny's illness, I made a commitment. I wanted very deeply to have a public way of declaring myself and my ministry once again to be under the complete control of Jesus Christ. A sense of cleansing and empowerment flooded through me as I received the prayers and love of my brethren for a new surrender of myself to the gospel ministry.

With that commitment, I realized I needed to examine very closely the journey I had taken and to think through very carefully what had happened to me. Why had I bought into this in the first place?

For a time, I questioned whether I had ever honestly and truly come to a real experience of new birth in Jesus Christ. Perhaps I had gotten so caught up in the spirit of Judi's family and her church that I had made a premature commitment in an emotional state, rather than genuinely turning away from ego and the world. We focused so much on that initial experience of conversion that perhaps we were not making disciples so much as we were manipulating decisions. I've come to believe that the church has suffered by attempting to separate the "decision" and "discipleship" dimensions of the faith. A complete reading of the New Testament seems to indicate that to focus on one of those twin poles of the Christian life to the exclusion of the other is only half a gospel, and there is no such thing as half a gospel.

I resolved, however, that my conversion had been complete in the dimension of decision. I have no doubt that I had experienced the new birth in Christ, and I have dismissed my questions about that. I did discover a couple of key points, though.

The discipleship dimension of my earliest days was lacking in sufficient depth. My outer Christian life in the fellowship was fine. There was a lot of acceptance and support for my surrender to a call to ministry as a pastor. My inner life where I was growing and maturing was not so terrific. I believe now that my roots were too shallow to survive the liberal environment.

Paul's charge to Timothy concerning the office of an overseer includes the stipulation that "he must not be a recent convert, or he may be puffed up with conceit and fall into the condemnation of the devil" (1 Tim. 3:6). I take that to mean that the ego can be a stumbling block to the recent convert.

There is a process that takes place when one comes to Jesus Christ and becomes a new person. Though we are new creatures in Christ, we still struggle with sin and the Devil, and a time of growth and maturity (discipleship) is critical so that the mind we bring to Christ may share in the mind of Christ. After the profession comes the process. That process was weak in my life and it was my ego that demanded a change in schools. Though there was a great deal within my fellowship I could point to as reasons for the change, the most honest conclusion I must draw now is that the primary issue had to do more with meeting my ego needs for approved educational credentials than it did with being faithful to my calling.

The issue of growth and maturity in the faith brought to the surface the critical issue of authority. Who or what is the authority in our Christian life?

I came to Christ and to the fellowship of the church in a way that changed my life. That church (for whatever reason God knows, I don't) was the authority God put in my life. The fellowship there, the commitment to biblical Christianity, the pastors, and the place it held in my life was crucial for my spiritual foundations. When I left that church, I did not replace its authority in my life with any other. I became my own authority and my own intellect provided the guidance for my spiritual life.

Authority, certainties, absolutes—these terms are utter anathema to the liberal mind. I had developed such an open mind that everything in it evaporated. Authority is essential in my life and in the rebuilding of the foundations for my ministry. It has become very clear to me that the issue is not rigid certainty vs. insecure uncertainty, but rather certainty built upon humility and grace.

Now these foundations undergird the joy of my faith. That there is a God whose desire is for the salvation of every human soul is the overriding absolute in my life.

The authority that nourishes that absolute is the biblical revelation and the fellowship of Jesus Christ and His people. The certainty that gives power to the joy of faith for me is that I know, ". . . Woe to me if I do not preach the gospel!" (1 Cor. 9:16).

What had seemed to me to be the very reasonable and rational step of examining every pillar in the foundation of my spiritual life was in reality only the trading of one authority for another. My original foundations were replaced with the authority of human rationality. It turns out that the master of the far country—human rationalism—is a devastating and cruel master indeed, who under the guise of the reasonable and rational offers only bondage to that which cannot redeem.

If you have been in that church where the human intellect is the real master, are in it, or are thinking of going to it, be sure that the time will come when you will (or perhaps you already have) say to yourself, "This is absolutely hollow and empty."

Another key in the rebuilding of the foundations was for me to recognize what is required when dealing with sin. The only way to begin the cure of sin is to turn one's life around and head for Christ and His church—repentance. My journey was not the harmless wanderings of a mischievous lad. It was purposeful turning to that which was not life, but death. The only way out is to turn around and go back home, back to the place where you left.

A part of my looking at the beginnings of my journey was to go back and do a bit of twenty-year-old undone homework. I wrote to the senior pastor of the church where I had first begun, to the man who signed my license to preach, offered guidance, encouragement, and a job so I could provide for my family. That letter read in part:

Dear Wendell,

This letter is twenty years late . . . it is a thank-you letter.

When I left the church so many years ago, I was hurt, angry, confused, and a bit lost. But there's something on my heart today.

I left without saying thank you. For the support, encouragement, love, and guidance . . . thank you from the bottom of my heart.

Somehow, in a way that is a mystery to me, I've managed to get home to the faith I once had.

In Christ,
John Jewell

Very early in my rebuilding process, I also went to see Truman, the former associate pastor of that church and the one who is now the pastor. His friendship has nourished my homecoming.

From my experience I came to see clearly the choice that faces contemporary Christianity. The theological spectrum runs from so far right to so far left that thousands of people find themselves quite confused by the array of church life available. There need not be that confusion. The choices are finally only two. Those choices are liberal humanism, which has become the mainstream of mainline Protestant church life, and biblical Christianity, reflected in the churches that hold to the evangelical spirit of the historic faith. Though the differences within each stream of church life are still marked, the choice is clear.

One choice places human wisdom and the rational process at the bottom-line. It is a basic trust in the rational abilities of humanity sufficient to bring about the salvation of mankind. Deception is rampant because one can espouse a love for Jesus Christ, a dedication to the Scriptures, and a reliance upon the Spirit of God, but the final authority in all matters is the rational, intellectual process. That choice, stripped of all religious trappings, stands naked as liberal humanism.

The other choice sees mankind as essentially lost without the direct intervention of God and redemption offered in Jesus Christ, and declares the mission of the church to proclaim the new birth and a life in Christ of salvation, worship, and service. That choice is biblical Christianity.

Let me speak bluntly. If you are in the process of heading for that distant land, I think you know within your heart that you are headed for a dry and thirsty place. The tip-off is that restless feeling that sits inside and gives you that twinge of anxiety you feel. I can only say that a time of not going anywhere is in order.

If you cannot honestly remain at home with the faith you have, take a sabbatical on your doubts rather than continuing the course on which you find yourself. Better yet, find a person you can trust with whom you can share the things that are going on inside you. Ask the Lord for someone who won't judge you or pronounce the wrath of God upon you for having spiritual turmoil—someone who has a degree of maturity in the Lord and who perhaps has struggled with his own faith. I offer my own story, not so much as a carte blanche pronouncement about how you should live your life, but as a testimony to the pain and misery that lies out there in the far country.

By God's grace I found my way home again. And by God's grace, Johnny found his way home—to stay. He came to a time of surrendering his own life to Jesus Christ for His service and went off to a school where Christ is honored and the regimen tough. Johnny struggled with his old nature in much the same way I did and took leave from school to develop his own discipline and earn his own funds to go to school. Though he still struggles, his life is a miracle. I am amazed every time I think of how his life was spared. He will, I am sure, one day tell his own story and passion to reach those whose lives are wrecked as his was.

If you are in famine right now and have given up hope of ever having your faith back, I can say it *is* possible to get home to a meaningful faith again. I tossed out my *whole* faith, along with some of the legalism and cultural trappings that accompanied the expression of the gospel. In talking with friends and colleagues along the way who shared much of my journey, it became clear that many people have assumed they cannot get back to a living faith in Christ, when it is really a particular church or practice that they cannot abide. The point is, you're hurting, and the only healing for that pain is the healing that comes through a surrender of all of life to Christ.

When we make the effort to turn toward home, the Father is right there, encouraging us along the way, and waiting with open arms.

> " '. . . bring the fatted calf and kill it, and let us eat and make merry; for this my son was dead, and is alive again; he was lost, and is found.' . . ." (Luke 15:24).

Notes

Chapter 6
1. Rudolph Bultmann, *Kerygma and Myth,* ed. Hans Werner Bartsch (New York: Harper and Row, 1961), p. 3.

Chapter 8
1. Harry Emerson Fosdick, *The Living of These Days* (New York: Harper and Bros., 1956), p. 52.
2. L. Harold DeWolf, *The Case for Theology in Liberal Perspective* (Philadelphia: Westminster Press, 1959), p. 17.
3. "Candid Conversation with the Evangelist," *Christianity Today,* July 17, 1981, pp. 18–24.

Chapter 11
1. Paul Tillich, *Systematic Theology* (Chicago: University of Chicago Press, 1967), p. 7.
2. Stephen Rose, *Who's Killing the Church?* (Chicago: Chicago Missionary Society, 1966), p. 125.
3. William Hamilton and Thomas Altizer, *The Death of God* (New York: Bobbs-Merrill Co., 1966), p. xii.

Chapter 12
1. Stephen Rose, *Alarms and Visions* (Chicago: Renewal Magazine, 1967), p. 128.
2. Ibid.

Chapter 16
1. Eugene O'Neill, *Long Day's Journey Into Night* (New Haven: Yale University Press, 1956), p. 173.